BASIC GRAMMAR GUIDE

BEGINNING Practice for Competency, Proficiency, and High School Equivalency Examinations

Sister Loretta (Agnes Ann) Pastva, S.N.D.

Department of English,
Cleveland Diocesan School System,
Cleveland, Ohio

**ARCO PUBLISHING, INC.
NEW YORK**

Credits:

p. 1, cartoon © 1975 by Malcolm Hancock, reprinted from *Saturday Review*; p. 3, left—courtesy American Craft Council, top—courtesy Bill Rase Productions, Inc., bottom—courtesy Norwegian National Tourist Office; p. 12, courtesy of Photo Division, CBS Television Network Press Information; p. 15, courtesy National Aeronautics and Space Administration (NASA); p. 17, Photo: courtesy of the French Government Tourist Office; p. 25, courtesy U.S. Department of Labor, Bureau of Labor Statistics; p. 34 and p. 35, courtesy of the U.S. Department of the Interior, National Park Service and the Swiss National Tourist Office; p. 40, casserole—courtesy Corning Glass Works, art show photo—courtesy of the French Government Tourist Office, rehearsal photo—Marianne Barcellona, New York Philharmonic; p. 41, courtesy of Oscar Mayer & Co., Kraft, Inc., Morton Salt Division of MortonNorwich, McCormick & Company, Inc., Best Foods, a division of CPC International, Inc., American Home Foods, USDA photograph by KNELL; p. 49, photographed at Corby-Leeds by Moshé Gelboim; p. 62, top left—courtesy of British Tourist Authority, top right—courtesy Con Edison, bottom—courtesy New York State Cooperative Extension, Agricultural News Service; p. 73, Photo: U.S. Department of Agriculture; p. 76, courtesy of the U.S. Department of the Interior, National Park Service; p. 79, left—courtesy Head Sports Wear, Inc., a subsidiary of AMF Inc., top—Allen Stewart, bottom—Photo: Marianne Barcellona, New York Philharmonic; p. 96, left—courtesy New York Yankees, right—Photo: courtesy of the New York City Department of Parks and Recreation; p. 97, courtesy Photo Division, CBS Television Network Press Information.

Published by Arco Publishing, Inc.
219 Park Avenue South, New York, N.Y. 10003

Copyright © 1982, 1976 by Sister Loretta (Agnes Ann) Pastva

Library of Congress Cataloging in Publication Data

Pastva, Loretta.
  Basic grammar guide—beginning practice for competency and proficiency exams.

  Previous ed. published under title: Signals.
  Includes index.
  1. English language—Grammar—1950–   I. Title.
PE1112.P34   1981   428.2   81-7934
ISBN 0-668-05464-6   (Library Edition)   AACR2
ISBN 0-668-05250-3   (Paper Edition)

Printed in the United States of America

Contents

Preface

Have you ever made any of the following remarks?

> "Writing frustrates me, but if I want to graduate (or get that job), I've got to at least learn the basics."
>
> "I wish I could learn to write better."
>
> "I have the ideas, but I don't know how to make them sound right on paper."
>
> "I like to write, but I'm not always sure about grammar and punctuation."

Whether you are a student, a homemaker, a factory worker, a doctor, lawyer or Indian chief, if any of these statements expresses something you've felt, the Arco *Basic Grammar Guides* are for you. These books are especially useful to those of you who must pass a high school competency or proficiency exam for graduation or advancement, or who are working toward a high school equivalency diploma or are involved in an adult basic education program.

Clear writing requires two kinds of skills: organizational (putting ideas into order) and conventional (getting ideas into a form that others can decode). Organizational skills can be learned in a variety of ways, including ordinary experience. The conventions—spelling, vocabulary, grammar, punctuation, and usage—must be studied and practiced. The Arco *Basic Grammar Guides* are a painless way to teach yourself the conventions of English.

These guides are different from most English handbooks because they teach only what you need to know to write better. They begin at the very beginning, taking nothing for granted, and progressively lead you to the required skills.

In using the guides you won't waste unnecessary time on theory for its own sake, or on rules you won't ever use. For instance, since no one says, "Give *he* the book," the indirect object pronoun is not developed. But because people *are* tempted to write, "They bought tickets for Miguel and *I*," the use of the object pronoun in compound forms is taught and tested.

Another advantage of the *Basic Grammar Guides* is that, unlike mail order courses or even classroom instruction where you must wait for test results, the guides provide instant answers to all exercises. The answer key at the back of each book allows you to check your answers while the questions are still fresh in your mind. And an answer key never grows impatient or is shocked, no matter how often it is consulted!

The Arco *Basic Grammar Guides* build all writing skills through simple, step-by-step instructions that are reinforced by exercises and drill. Hints for vocabulary development go beyond rote memorization of isolated words. The guides concentrate on troublesome words, but also suggest lifetime habits of vocabulary improvement and teach full use of dictionary skills. Because formal grammar and usage are not always appropriate in daily conversation, the guides present alternatives of usage levels. But since in the world of work and education, writing usually demands greater formality than speaking, the guides emphasize standard usage. In the chapters on punctuation, capitalization, and spelling, you will find clearly defined rules, explanations of the logic behind each rule, and suggestions to help you remember the rules you need to know. A thorough index will help you find what you need in a hurry.

How to Use the Guides

You will notice that the Arco *Basic Grammar Guides* contain a minimum of explanatory material. The fundamentals of language and the conventions of English are best learned through concise instruction—often just a few simple rules—and through practice.

What Order? Any chapter in the book can be used independently or in any sequence. You may wish to begin on page one and work straight through to the last page, or you may find it interesting to work at a few items in several chapters simultaneously before completing any one chapter. You will find margin references to other sections of the text that concern whatever is being taught. If, for example, you decide to study the spelling lesson on the plural of nouns, and feel that you need a review of nouns, you will find a reference to the page that teaches you how to identify nouns. The subject matter is also identified at the top of each page for easy reference.

Level of Difficulty Since each guide is self-contained, nothing is assumed. Background information is reviewed in each book. The difficulty of material increases with each book, however. *Beginning Practice for Competency, Proficiency and High School Equivalency Examinations* concentrates on the most basic areas of English, giving much time to the most common writing errors. *Intermediate Practice for Competency, Proficiency and High School Equivalency Examinations* does further work on fundamentals, but adds new information. *Advanced Practice for Competency, Proficiency and High School Equivalency Examinations* covers all skills needed for good writing, including research procedures. It also contains an Index to Usage and Style.

Original Writing Photographs and certain exercises are intended to stimulate original writing—your own compound sentences, for instance. These allow you to put your developing writing skills into practice, and can also serve as a springboard to more extensive writing.

Language Understanding and Enrichment Features titled "The Latest Thing" show how language and usage change with time. They too may suggest ideas for original writing.

Introduction

Rewrite this sentence as a question.

Peter Benchley wrote *Jaws*.

Now consider what you have done. You have:

1. Introduced a new word at the beginning of the sentence, the auxiliary *do*.

2. Added the mark of the past tense to the auxiliary by making it *did*.

3. Removed the mark of the past tense from *wrote* by changing it to *write*, the simple form.

4. Introduced a new mark of punctuation at the end to show that this sentence is to be read with an uplift of the voice at the end.

Did you know that you were performing all these sophisticated grammatical changes? Of course not. Changing a statement to a question is something you do easily and quickly without thinking about how to do it. If you are studying a foreign language, you know that question-asking operates differently in other languages. In Spanish, for instance, you would write:

Peter Benchley escribió *Jaws*.

and make these changes for a question:

¿Escribió *Jaws* Peter Benchley?

Because you need to ask questions all the time, you learned how to ask them almost as soon as you learned to talk. But you never needed to explain what you were doing, and you probably never will. It is enough that you are capable of using language intelligently.

Although you can perform the basic operations of communication without thinking, there are certain things about language that probably always make you stop. For example, make a choice here:

(he, him)   His brother and _____ left on the noon plane.

If you're speaking to a friend, the choice is not even important. Your friend will understand you, no matter which word you choose. But if you're writing, you know you have to be careful. One word is "right" and the other is "wrong." The choice you make marks you as a careful writer or as an ignorant person.

This book is designed to give you the information and practice you need to make just the right choices, especially where you have the most trouble – in writing.

WORDS ARE POWER

Indeed they are. The more words you know, the closer you are to making your language work for you. How do you learn words? Here are some ways to build your stockpile of power words.

1

Be a Reader

Reading is an easy way to build your word stockpile. Unless you read books that are too easy for you, you will meet many new words. Often you can tell their meaning from the words around them.

> "Hooper said there was one thing we could do," Meadows said. "Now that you've got the beaches closed down, we could chum. You know, spread fish guts and goodies like that around in the water. If there's a shark around, he said, that will bring him running."

Did you know the word *chum* and its meaning before you read this paragraph? How has the author defined it? Why do you think the author gave the definition?

A definition or explanation of an unfamiliar word will sometimes precede or follow the word, as it does for *chum*. If the author does not give a definition, you can sometimes figure out the meaning from the situation, at least in a general way.

> Cinderella's sisters were vain and petty, cross and petulant, haughty and mean and selfish. Cinderella, on the other hand, was completely altruistic.

Which qualities are bad, which good? How can you tell? Which words that you know give you an idea of what the unfamiliar words mean? Even if you don't know the meaning of *altruistic*, what guess can you make at its meaning? What other words does it contrast with? The next time you meet the word, it will at least mean something good. Of course, the best thing to do is look the word up in a dictionary and make a note of it.

List five new words that you have learned recently through reading. Did you get a general or specific idea of their meaning?

Be a Specialist

Everyone has a favorite hobby or interest. Usually you know many words about that subject. The following paragraph was composed around a special topic. Read the paragraph and write a title that sums up the topic. Define each of the italicized words either directly or by using it in a sentence.

Excerpt from *Jaws* by Peter Benchley, © 1974 by Peter Benchley. Reprinted by permission of Doubleday & Company, Inc.

The *witch* bowed *ceremoniously* to the *warlock* before muttering her *eerie incantations* over the blazing fire that lit the trees of the dark forest. Seemingly out of the darkness, she produced a *poppet* which she first beat with a gleaming *amulet* and then waved wildly in mid-air, tearing it to shreds. The *wizard* joined her in a *cackling* duet while the fire gradually died to leave the *forest* black as before.

Write a paragraph using a number of words from any topic you are very familiar with. Use one of these pictures for ideas.

Be A Dictionary Addict

Your very best aid for writing is the *dictionary*. Malcolm X taught himself to read and write by copying page after page from the dictionary. With a dictionary at your elbow, you can be a better writer today because at a moment's notice, you can find all the following information about a word:

correct *spelling*

word *division*

correct *pronunciation*

part of *speech*

word *changes* and *grammar* pointers

mechanics—capitalization, underlining and hyphenating

word *history*

appropriate *usage*

meanings, including *synonyms* and sometimes *antonyms*

A good dictionary can do more than supply information about words. Browse through your dictionary.

1. Look at the Table of Contents and the Guide to the Use of the Dictionary, and make a list of all the kinds of information you can find besides definitions.
2. Write down any items that you were surprised to find in your dictionary. Which interested you in particular?
3. How many pages does your dictionary have? How many words does it include? What year was it published? (Look on the back of the title page.)

If you don't already have a good dictionary, get one. But just having a dictionary is not enough. It should become one of your best friends. You should read all the introductory notes and explanations, examine it carefully and get to know it like the back of your hand.

All dictionaries list words alphabetically. If you know the alphabet, you will be able to find a word easily. How fast can you arrange the following words in alphabetical order:

| deep | gene | case | zinnia | hoax |
| astrodome | smoggy | rope | undulation | playback |

The following words all have the same beginning letter; arrange them alphabetically by the second, third or fourth letters.

Example: date, duct, duteous, dutiable, dutiful

Da comes before **du. Duc** comes before **dut. Te** comes before **ti. Tia** comes before **tif.**

A	B	C	D	E
courser	moccasin	rootless	stickleback	traitor
coursing	muddle	rut	stickle	tramcar
courtesan	medium	radiate	stick out	traject
courteous	myrtle	refine	stickpin	traitorous
court	mask	realism	stickman	trajectory
courtesy	mist	roadster	stickler	tram

Searching Out Spelling

For more on unsounded letters, see page 100.

When someone tells you to find the correct spelling in the dictionary, your first question is probably: How can I look up the spelling if I don't know how to spell the word?

Sometimes pronunciation will not be a help. You must memorize the sound of certain letter combinations. Some of these letter combinations and examples of words in which they occur are:

ps	(s)	psychology	ph	(f)	philosophy
pn	(n)	pneumonia	acq	(ak)	acquaintance
mn	(n)	mnemonics	ch	(k)	chorus
kn	(n)	knowledge	gh	(g)	ghetto

Give another example for each sound.

Good spellers can usually recognize a misspelled word. Decide which words from this list are wrong, then find the correct spelling in your dictionary.

recieve	yeild	alright	Massiah
syanide	proffesor	pasturize	skorching
axident	firey	shadow	eerry
pyscology	squeal	analyse	drownded
carasel	alussion	bizness	killn

See page 102 for spelling plurals.

Find the spelling of the plural form of the following:

fly	money	*tour de force*
man	sheep	kine
datum	kink	hero

These abbreviations identify different kinds of verbs—transitive and intransitive. You will study them when you get to page 36.

Find the spelling of the past tense of the following verbs. Be sure to look at the verb, which is followed by *vb*, *vi* **or** *vt*, **not at the noun, which is followed by** *n*.

control	duel	may	can
sneak	swing	freeze	break
dive	picnic	tread	shred

Probing for Pronunciation

Sometimes you have to read aloud. You need to know the correct pronunciation of words you are not sure of. Every dictionary includes a complete guide to pronunciation near its beginning. For handy reference it often includes a *key to pronunciation* at the bottom of the page. This key uses words that everyone is familiar with to indicate the phonetic sounds. Does the key in your dictionary occur on every page or only on every other page?

An important thing to notice is how your dictionary marks stressed syllables. Some dictionaries use a raised stress mark before the syllable to be given first stress. A dropped stress mark before the syllable indicates a secondary stress in a longer word.

falcon ˈfal·kən   falderol ˈfäl·də·ˌräl

Some dictionaries place accent marks after the syllables to be stressed, using heavier and lighter stress marks to indicate primary and secondary stress.

fallible falʹ·li·ble   voodooistic vooʹ·doo·isʹ·tic

Say each word slowly to discover syllables.

Divide into syllables and mark the primary and secondary accents of the following words.

umbrella	perfect (v)	admirable	infamous
posthumous	impotent	combatant	pentameter
perfume (n)	irrevocable	fillet	mischievous
perfume (v)	affluence	finale	orography
perfect (adj)	advertisement	exquisite	Yom Kippur

Use the key to pronunciation at the bottom of the dictionary pages to find the first pronunciation given for the following words or parts of words underlined.

quay	rhymes with	me or stay?
calm	rhymes with	alma or bomb?

bade	rhymes with	lad or made?
often	rhymes with	coffin or soft ten?
posterior	rhymes with	gospel or host?
steppe	rhymes with	pep or leap?
data	rhymes with	late or that?
respite	rhymes with	tight or kit?

Study the sample dictionary on pages 8 and 9. Decide which meaning of *light* would apply in the following sentences. Answer by writing the entry number, the important variant number, the minor variant letter and the definition or synonym after the colon.

Example: Would you *light* the way down the stairs?
³light 2a : conduct with a light : GUIDE

1. Her *light* conduct is responsible for her poor grades.
2. Bruce has the *light* coloring of his mother.
3. Star*light*, star bright . . .
4. The cavalry officer *lighted* at the General's headquarters.
5. The candy company was cited for selling *light* pounds.
6. Jodi suddenly saw the *light*. She understood at last.
7. The coverup finally came to *light*.
8. The *light* was emerging softly in the east.
9. Henry was a very *light* sleeper.
10. She felt *light* from lack of food.
11. They set out for an evening of *light* entertainment.
12. The merry-go-round left the children feeling *light*.
13. Harvey *lit* into his steak with gusto.
14. They served *light* drinks to celebrate her birthday.
15. His tap on the door was timid, *light*.

1 Notice that there are six separate entries for different meanings of "light." The most common definitions are usually given first.

2 The part of speech, or word class, of each word is given in italics right after the pronunciation. In this dictionary, the abbreviations are: *n*-noun, *vb*-verb, *vt*-transitive verb, *vi*-intransitive verb, *adj*-adjective, *adv*-adverb.

3 In addition to the six different entries for "light," there are, you can see, seventeen numbered variations of the adjective "light." The first variation has four minor variations of its own, lettered a, b, c and d.

4 Here you see that there are two ways to form the past tense of the verb "light." By giving you examples, the dictionary shows you the context in which the form "lit" is used.

5 The words in italics tell you that the expression "light bread" is colloquial —used mainly in the South and Midland areas of the country.

6 Other verb forms are given after the main form. If you want to find out how to spell "lightening," you must look under the simple form, "lighten."

7 This entry shows six different meanings for the adverb "lightly." The words in capital letters are synonyms for "lightly." Notice that the dictionary also gives you an example of how the word is commonly used. The symbol ~ substitutes for the word.

8 Guide words at the top of each page tell you the first and last words on the page.

---

8   light ● limbos

1 ¹light \'līt\ *n* [ME, fr. OE *lēoht*; akin to OHG *lioht* light, L *luc-*, *lux* light, *lucēre* to shine, Gk *leukos* white] **1 a :** something that makes vision possible **b :** the sensation aroused by stimulation of the visual receptors : BRIGHTNESS **c :** an electromagnetic radiation in the wavelength range including infrared, visible, ultraviolet, and X rays and traveling in a vacuum with a speed of about 186,281 miles per second; *specif :* the part of this range that is visible to the human eye **2 a :** DAYLIGHT **b :** DAWN **3 :** a source of light: as **a :** a celestial body **b :** CANDLE **c :** an electric light **4** *archaic* **:** SIGHT **4a 5 a :** spiritual illumination **b :** INNER LIGHT **c :** ENLIGHTENMENT **d :** TRUTH **6 a :** public knowledge <facts brought to ~> **b :** a particular aspect or appearance presented to view <now saw the matter in a different ~> **7 :** a particular illumination **8 :** something that enlightens or informs <he shed some ~ on the problem> **9 :** a medium (as a window or windowpane) through which light is admitted **10** *pl* **:** a set of principles, standards, or opinions <worship according to one's ~s —Adrienne Koch> **11 :** a noteworthy person in a particular place or field : LUMINARY **12 :** a particular expression of the eye **13 a :** LIGHTHOUSE. BEACON **b (1) :** TRAFFIC SIGNAL **(2) :** a green traffic light **14 :** the representation of light in art **15 :** a flame for lighting something — **in the light of 1 :** from the point of view of **2** *or* **in light of :** in view of

2 ²light *adj* **1 :** having light : BRIGHT <a ~ airy room> **2 a :** not dark, intense, or swarthy in color or coloring : PALE **b** *of colors* **:** medium in saturation and high in lightness <~ blue> **3** *of coffee* **:** served with cream or milk

³light *vb* **light·ed** *or* **lit** \'līt\; **light·ing** *vi* **1 :** to become light : BRIGHTEN — usu. used with *up* <her face *lit* up> **2 :** to take fire **3 :** to ignite something (as a cigarette) — often used with *up* ~ *vt* **1 :** to set fire to **2 a :** to conduct with a light : GUIDE **b :** ILLUMINATE <rockets ~ up the sky> **c :** ANIMATE. BRIGHTEN <a smile *lit* up her face>
syn LIGHT. KINDLE. IGNITE. FIRE *shared meaning element* : to start something to burn

3 ⁴light *adj* [ME, fr. OE *lēoht;* akin to OHG *lihti* light, L *levis*, Gk *elachys* small] **1 a :** having little weight : not heavy **b :** designed to carry a comparatively small load <a ~ truck> **c :** having relatively little weight in proportion to bulk <aluminum is a ~ metal> **d :** containing less than the legal, standard, or usual weight <a ~ coin> **2 a :** of little importance : TRIVIAL **b :** not abundant : SCANTY <~ rain> **3 a :** easily disturbed <a ~ sleeper> **b :** exerting a minimum of force or pressure : GENTLE <a ~ touch> **c :** resulting from a very slight pressure : FAINT <~ print> **4 a :** easily endurable <a ~ illness> **b :** requiring little effort <~ work> **5 :** capable of moving swiftly or nimbly <~ on his feet> **6 a :** FRIVOLOUS <~ conduct> **b :** lacking in stability : CHANGEABLE <~ opinions> **c :** sexually promiscuous **7 :** free from care : CHEERFUL **8 :** intended chiefly to entertain <~ verse> **9 a :** having a comparatively low alcoholic content <~ wines> **b :** having a relatively mild flavor **10 a :** easily digested <~ soup> **b :** well leavened <a ~ crust> **11 :** lightly armed or equipped <~ cavalry> **12 :** coarse and sandy or easily pulverized <~ soil> **13 :** DIZZY. GIDDY <felt ~ in the head> **14 a :** carrying little or no cargo <the ship returned ~> **b :** producing goods for direct consumption by the consumer <~ industry> **15 :** not bearing a stress or accent <a ~ syllable> **16 :** having a clear soft quality <a ~ voice> **17 :** being in debt to the pot in a poker game <three chips ~> — **light·ish** \-ish\ *adj*

⁵light *adv* **1 :** LIGHTLY **2 :** with little baggage <travel ~>

4 ⁶light *vi* **light·ed** *or* **lit** \'līt\; **light·ing** [ME *lighten*, fr. OE *lihtan;* akin to OE *lēoht* light in weight] **1 :** DISMOUNT **2 :** SETTLE. ALIGHT <a bird *lit* on the lawn> **3 :** to fall unexpectedly **4 :** to arrive by chance : HAPPEN <*lit* upon a solution> — **light into :** to attack forcefully <I *lit into* that food until I'd finished off the heel of the loaf —Helen Eustis>

5 **light air** *n* **:** wind having a speed of 1 to 3 miles per hour
light bread \'līt-ˌbred\ *n* [²*light*] *chiefly South & Midland* **:** bread in loaves made from white flour leavened with yeast

6 ¹light·en \'līt-ᵊn\ *vb* **light·ened; light·en·ing** \'līt-niŋ, -ᵊn-iŋ\ [ME *lightenen*, fr. *light*] *vt* **1 :** to make light or clear : ILLUMINATE **2** *archaic* **:** ENLIGHTEN **3 :** to make (as a color) lighter ~ *vi* **1 a :** to shine brightly **b :** to grow lighter : BRIGHTEN **2 :** to give out flashes of lightning — **light·en·er** \'līt-nər, -ᵊn-ər\ *n*
²lighten *vb* **light·ened; light·en·ing** \'līt-niŋ, -ᵊn-iŋ\ *vt* **1 a :** to relieve of a burden in whole or in part <the news ~ed his mind> **b :** to reduce in weight or quantity : LESSEN <~ his duties> **c :** to make less wearisome : ALLEVIATE <~ his sorrow> **2 :** CHEER. GLADDEN *vi* **1 :** to become lighter or less burdensome **2 :** to become more cheerful <his mood ~ed> *syn* see RELIEVE — **light·en·er** \'līt-nər, -ᵊn-ər\ *n*

7 light·ly \'līt-lē\ *adv* **1 :** with little weight or force : GENTLY **2 :** in a small degree or amount <~ salted food> **3 :** with little difficulty : EASILY **4 :** in an agile manner : NIMBLY. SWIFTLY **5 :** with indifference or carelessness : UNCONCERNEDLY <the problem should not be passed over ~ —Shelly Halpern> **6 :** GAILY. CHEERFULLY <offenses not ~ forgiven>

light·ness \-nəs\ *n* **1 :** the quality or state of being illuminated : ILLUMINATION **2 :** the attribute of object colors by which the object appears to reflect or transmit more or less of the incident light

666

²light·ness *n* **1** : the quality or state of being light in weight **2** : lack of seriousness and stability of character often accompanied by casual heedlessness **3 a** : the quality or state of being nimble **b** : an ease and gaiety of style or manner **4** : a lack of weightiness or force : DELICACY

9 *syn* LIGHTNESS, LEVITY, FRIVOLITY, FLIPPANCY, VOLATILITY *shared meaning element* : gaiety or indifference where seriousness and attention are called for *ant* seriousness

14 **¹like·ly** \'lī-klē\ *adj* **like·li·er; -est** [ME, fr. ON *glíkligr,* fr. *glíkr* like; akin to OE *gelic*] **1** : of such a nature or circumstance as to make something probable <~ of success> **2 a** : RELIABLE, CREDIBLE <a ~ enough story> **b** : having a high probability of occurring or being true : very probable **3** : apparently qualified : SUITABLE <a ~ place> **4** : PROMISING <a ~ subject> **5** : ATTRACTIVE <a ~ child> *syn* see PROBABLE *ant* unlikely

10 **like-mind·ed** \'līk-'mīn-dəd\ *adj* : having a like disposition or purpose : of the same mind or habit of thought — **like-mind·ed-ly** *adv* — **like-mind·ed·ness** *n*

11 **like·ness** \'līk-nəs\ *n* **1** : the quality or state of being like : RESEMBLANCE **2** : APPEARANCE, SEMBLANCE **3** : COPY, PORTRAIT *syn* LIKENESS, SIMILARITY, RESEMBLANCE, SIMILITUDE, ANALOGY, AFFINITY *shared meaning element* : agreement or correspondence in details (as of appearance, structure, or quality) *ant* unlikeness

lik·ing \'lī-kiŋ\ *n* : favorable regard : FONDNESS, TASTE <had a greater ~ for law —E. M. Coulter> <took a ~ to the newcomer>

li·lac \'lī-lək, -ˌlak, -ˌläk\ *n* [obs. F (now *lilas*), fr. Ar *līlak,* fr. Per *nīlak* bluish, fr. *nīl* blue, fr. Skt *nīla* dark blue] **1 a** : a European shrub (*Syringa vulgaris*) of the olive family that is often an escape in No. America and has cordate ovate leaves and large panicles of fragrant pink-purple flowers **b** : a tree or shrub congeneric with the lilac **2** : a variable color averaging a moderate purple

12 **lil·i·a·ceous** \ˌlil-ē-'ā-shəs\ *adj* : of or relating to lilies or the lily family

lilac 1a

Lil·ith \'lil-əth\ *n* [LHeb *lilith,* fr. Heb, a female demon] **1** : a female figure who in rabbinic legend is Adam's first wife, is supplanted by Eve, and becomes an evil spirit **2** : a famous witch in medieval demonology

lil·li·put \'lil-i-(ˌ)pət\ *n, often cap* : LILLIPUTIAN

13 **¹lil·li·pu·tian** \ˌlil-ə-'pyü-shən\ *adj, often cap* **1** : of, relating to, or characteristic of the Lilliputians or the island of Lilliput **2 a** : SMALL, MINIATURE **b** : PETTY

²Lilliputian *n* **1** : an inhabitant of an island in Swift's *Gulliver's Travels* who is six inches tall **2** *often not cap* : one resembling a Lilliputian; *esp* : an undersized individual

¹lily \'lil-ē\ *n, pl* **lil·ies** [ME *lilie,* fr. OE, fr. L *lilium*] **1** : any of a genus (*Lilium* of the family Liliaceae, the lily family) of erect perennial leafy-stemmed bulbous herbs that are native to the northern hemisphere and are widely cultivated for their showy flowers; *broadly* : any of various plants of the lily family or of the related amaryllis or iris families **2** : any of various plants with showy flowers: as **a** : a scarlet anemone (*Anemone coronaria*) that grows wild in Palestine **b** : WATER LILY **c** : CALLA **3** : FLEUR-DE-LIS 2

15 **²lily** *adj* : resembling a lily in fairness, purity, or fragility <my lady's ~ hand —John Keats>

16 **¹limb** \'lim\ *n* [ME *lim,* fr. OE; akin to ON *limr* limb, L *limes* limit, *limen* threshold, Gk *leimōn* meadow] **1** : one of the projecting paired appendages (as wings) of an animal body used esp. for movement and grasping but sometimes modified into sensory or sexual organs; *esp* : a leg or arm of a human being **2** : a large primary branch of a tree **3** : an active member or agent **4** : EXTENSION, BRANCH **5** : a mischievous child — **limbed** \'limd\ *adj* — **limb·less** \'lim-ləs\ *adj* — **limby** \'lim-ē\ *adj* — **out on a limb** : in an exposed or dangerous position with little chance of retreat

²limb *vt* : DISMEMBER; *esp* : to cut off the limbs of (a felled tree)

¹lim·bo \'lim-(ˌ)bō\ *n, pl* **limbos** [ME, fr. ML, abl. of *limbus* limbo, fr. L, border — more at LIMP] **1** *often cap* : an abode of souls that are according to Roman Catholic theology barred from heaven because of not having received Christian baptism **2 a** : a place or state of restraint or confinement **b** : a place or state of neglect or oblivion <proposals kept in ~> **c** : an intermediate or transitional place or state

²limbo *n, pl* **limbos** [native name in West Indies] : a West Indian acrobatic dance orig. for men that involves bending over backwards and passing under a horizontal pole lowered slightly for each successive pass

ə abut	ᵊ kitten	ər further	a back	ā bake	ä cot, cart
aů out	ch chin	e less	ē easy	g gift	i trip
j joke	ŋ sing	ō flow	ȯ flaw	ȯi coin	th thin
ü loot	ů foot	y yet	yü few	yů furious	zh vision

---

9 At the end of the entry, the dictionary sometimes gives you synonyms and directs you to other words which may suggest more synonyms or antonyms for "lightness."

10 If you need to know when to put a hyphen in a word, the dictionary shows you. Follow the dictionary style to decide whether a word is hyphenated, two separate words or one compound word.

11 The pronunciation of a word is shown in slant lines immediately following the word. A key for pronouncing each sound is at the bottom of every other page.

12 Pictures and charts of some items are features of many dictionaries. Look up the word "alphabet" in your own dictionary.

13 The note *often cap* tells you that this word is often written with a capital letter.

14 All dictionaries enter words by their main forms and shown the word divided into syllables. Small dots separate the syllables.

15 To show you how a word has been used, this dictionary gives you brief quotations. The quotation here is from the poet John Keats; it helps you see how "lily" can be used as an adjective.

16 The history of a word is often part of a dictionary entry. This one, for example, tells you that the word "limb" comes from Middle English (ME) and Old English (OE); that there is a similar word in Old Norse (ON) with the same meaning; and that there is a relationship to the Latin (L) word for "threshold" and the Greek (Gk) word for "meadow." Knowing the history of a word can sometimes give you a clearer idea of its meaning.

By permission. From *Webster's New Collegiate Dictionary* © 1980 by G. & C. Merriam Co., Publishers of the Merriam-Webster Dictionaries.

All the italicized words in the sentences below have more than one definition. Use your dictionary to decide which definition fits the context. If the word is slang or colloquial, indicate that before your definition. Write a sentence with any of the other meanings.

1. The question *threw* him.
2. The queen's *suite* disbanded as soon as the procession ended.
3. The staff had to return the *dummy* by 5 p.m.
4. The boxer had a *cauliflower* ear.
5. His rent covers bed, *board* and lodging.
6. The gypsy *rooked* me when I went to have my palm read.
7. Will Leavers is a regular *chameleon*.
8. Skipper covered the little girl with a *throw*.
9. After the wedding he was a little *tight*.
10. Jenny *sailed into* her little sister.
11. Your *flummery* will not win you my consent.
12. After the robbery they divied the *jack* and went underground.
13. Are there any likely hitters on the *farm*?
14. He likes to *play* with people's emotions.
15. Martha Washington set the fad for *poke* bonnets.

Sorting Out Synonyms

As you can see by the entries for *light*, words may have many shades of meaning, some of which are expressed in synonyms. A synonym is a word that has the same or almost the same meaning as another word.

What synonyms do you find listed for these words? If your dictionary does not list them, look them up in an unabridged version. Write a sentence with the original word as well as with one of its synonyms. From your sentences show that you know the slight distinctions between them.

likely	native	fancy	kill
predilection	taste	invent	lack
serious	victory	cry	juncture
cure	quick	irascible	unruly
end	oppose	join	erase

Choose all the synonyms for any of the given words and write sentences that show you know their exact meanings.

In each of the following, one word is not a synonym. Identify the misfit.

1. abandon, island, desert, forsake, leave
2. breathed, sighed, cried, hissed, snorted
3. climbed, mounted, struggled up, jumped, ascended
4. light, feathery, airy, foamy, weightless, substantial
5. grate, honk, toot, blast, beep

Which words are needed for the context of each paragraph?

new recent fresh contemporary mod

The young couple's __1__ purchase was a __2__ ranch that needed only a __3__ coat of paint to make it look like __4__ .

walked ambled shuffled strode scurried

Lazy Ella __1__ noisily back and forth across the room until Uncle Henry rose from his chair and vigorously __2__ out. The children then emerged from their corners and __3__ about underfoot while Grandma __4__ over to the teakettle to pour some water.

tall gigantic big lanky

Ezra was __1__ and __2__ while his brother was __3__ boned and though shorter, gave the appearance of a __4__ tractor ready to roll over you.

Pick the *best* word for each sentence. Use each word only once.

healthy thriving flourishing blooming vigorous

1. The fertilizer produced blooms that were unbelievably _____ .
2. Ethel, her cheeks red from the piercing wind and her eyes sparkling like dew, gave the impression of a _____ rose.
3. Julie's unfailing sense of humor was one sign of her wonderfully _____ mind.
4. _____ his colorful hat, the clown threw tearful kisses to the audience.
5. Horns beeping, crowds jamming the intersections, police blowing their whistles, trucks and buses rattling their exhausts—all give evidence of a _____ metropolis.

LANGUAGE THAT COUNTS

Have you ever picketed for a cause you believe in? Then you know the power of language. A few strong words on a sign can say more than a twenty-minute speech. What matters is knowing how to put those words together.

Do you always get your meaning across? Do people sometimes misunderstand you or take what you've said the wrong way? Have you ever said, "I know what I want to say, but I just don't know how to say it!"

That's why you study language, English specifically, so you can learn to make your meaning clear. In order to manage your language, you have to know a few basic terms. You should be able to recognize—and talk about—the kinds of words you use and the way they work.

Without thinking about it, you talk in sentences. You don't talk nonsense unless you have a fever or are emotionally disturbed. You shouldn't have trouble rearranging the following words to make sentences. Do not change the form of any word.

Paints Jeffrey.   A flies robin.

Fly robins.   Their talks parakeet.

As they are printed, none of the word groups are sentences. How did you make them into sentences? Look at two more sentences.

Jeffrey paints Monica.   Monica paints Jeffrey.

Even though the words in both these sentences are exactly the same, the position of the words gives two completely different meanings. In English, word order determines sentence sense. Not all languages work that way.

You recognize that in English, groups of words make sense when they have a subject and a predicate. The subject is a word or group of words that names the idea or performer or action of the sentence. The predicate tells what the subject is doing. The smallest sense-making group of words is a sentence. It can be formed by a subject and a predicate of one word each.

Write a predicate that will say something about each of these subjects.

Example: Her book   fell.
            Subject (given)   Predicate

1. Genevieve   6. Their club   11. This skunk
2. The queen   7. That pianist   12. Edgar
3. A guitarist   8. My cousin   13. The boat
4. Her eyes   9. His pen   14. Roads
5. The radio   10. My feet   15. The minister

Supply a subject for each of these predicates.

Example: The child   screamed.
            Subject   Predicate (given)

1. drowned.   6. arrived.   11. squealed.
2. starve.   7. retreated.   12. passes.
3. overslept.   8. danced.   13. walked.
4. behaved.   9. voted.   14. practiced.
5. sings.   10. quarreled.   15. coughed.

No matter what other words you add to the thirty sentences you just made up, the subject and predicate will stay the same.

Her battered *book fell*.

Her precious and expensive *book fell*.

Because of its size, her *book fell* noisily.

Her *book fell* to the ground with a dull thud.

Her *book fell* right out of her hands onto the floor.

Change any three sentences you wrote in as many ways as you can, keeping the same subject and predicate. Underline the subject and predicate in each.

The subject is the noun that answers the question: Who or What performs the main action of the sentence?

_____ kneaded the dough for wheat bread.
(Who kneaded the dough?)

_____ set it on the range to rise.
(Who set it?)

_____ baked it in one hour.
(What baked it?)

Much later, _____ came in to eat it.
(Who came in?)

The predicate tells what the action is.

Rachel _____ her dog.
(What did she do?)

The cow _____ over the moon.
(What did the cow do?)

In each of the following sentences, either a subject or a predicate is missing. Supply whichever you think is needed. After your sentence write *S* if you supplied a subject, *P* if a predicate.

Example: 1. All morning _____ prepared for the party.
        1. Josie — S

1. Lem _____ out to the field with his dog.
2. A few minutes earlier _____ had barked insistently at the door.
3. _____ suspected an accident in the field.
4. Out of breath, he _____ at Abe's side.

5. Abe _____ something too low to be heard.

6. I _____ a fascinating book.

7. _____ you _____ any lately?

8. Yes, _____ enjoyed *Pride and Prejudice*.

9. Jane Austen _____ it.

10. _____ haven't read anything by Austen.

Write an exchange of brief sentences between these two people. Underline the subject and predicate in each sentence.

NOUNS COME FIRST

The sentence is the basic unit of communication in English. You have shown that you understand what makes a sentence; you can recognize subjects and predicates. The most important element of the subject is a noun; the key word in the predicate is a verb. You can't go much further without knowing how nouns and verbs work and what they are.

You can recognize nouns easily because they often come after determiners. While there are more nouns than anyone can count, there are only a few determiners. It is easy just to memorize the determiners. They fall into four groups.

1. **Articles:** an, a, the

2. **Possessive pronouns:** my, your, his, her, its, our, their

3. **Demonstrative pronouns:** this, that, these, those

4. **Numerals:** one, ten, thirty-five, etc.

There are two kinds of articles: **definite:** *the* book, *the* afghan; and **indefinite:** *a* book, *an* afghan.

The can be used before any noun, but *a* is used only before words that begin with a consonant. *An* is used before words that begin with *a, e, i, o,* short *u* and unsounded *h: a* building, *an* honest answer.

Supply *a* or *an* before each of the following nouns.

horse	emerald	xylophone	old camera
umbrella	igloo	acid	new radio
bush	hospital	aging cat	pair of stockings
hour	picnic	stocking	holey stocking
apple	radio	camera	honest man

Write sentences using these words.

heavenly feeling, hexagon, high cloud, hint, honor, human, horrible face, homage, hombre, honesty, honorable, apricot, councilman, eerie, forest, evil eye, imp, ostrich, biscuit, utterly fascinating story, animal, unbelievable, adventure, grotesque statue

Another useful way to recognize nouns is by inflections. **Inflections** are endings you can add to change the meaning of a noun in two ways:

From singular to plural add *-s* or *-es*
        one dog, ten million dog**s**

From plain to possessive add *'s* or just *'*
        the dog**'s** bone   singular
        the dog**s'** bones   plural

There are more details on spelling plurals on page 102 and following.

Once again, this is something you have been doing all your life. You follow a few simple rules, although you may not even know the rules. If a singular noun ends in *s, ch, x,* or *sh,* add *-es* to make it plural; otherwise add only *-s.* Write the plural form of the following nouns.

wish	search	voyage	axe	plant
word	earphone	trip	play	itch

The singular possessive is simpler yet, just *'s;* if a noun is already plural—has an s on the end—add only the apostrophe. Make the following nouns possessive.

Example: dog (bone) = dog's bone

child (cat)   telephone (ring)
cats (paws)   animals (skins)
books (bindings)   elephant (tusk)
plant (leaves)   Ray (glasses)
teacher (shoes)   Smiths (house)

Plural nouns may or may not be preceded by determiners. Tell when determiners in the following sentences should be used, or could be used but are not required. If no determiner is needed, indicate "zero determiner."

1. _____ cartons of _____ books were carried into _____ school.
2. _____ apples under _____ trees were rotting.
3. _____ new leather gloves had a tear in them.
4. Michael told Santa he wanted _____ toys for Christmas.
5. _____ leather coats are warmer than _____ worsted ones.

Study the picture and write the nouns you see. Look around you. Add other nouns.

For each noun below write a sentence. Make any five nouns possessive, five more plural. Use at least five determiners. If a word is not a noun, don't write a sentence for it.

1. paper	6. building	11. jump	16. beautiful
2. honor	7. South	12. aerial	17. ashtray
3. Hello	8. Gulf Road	13. obedience	18. gentlemen
4. Jack Smith	9. mug	14. of	19. wall
5. boy	10. hit	15. since	20. bedroom

Identify the nouns in this paragraph. Tell whether they are singular or plural and identify any determiners.

Jack crept around the side of the house. The wind whistled through the crisp fall leaves as he jumped softly onto a ledge. When he got his balance, he slowly stretched to raise his eyes just above the window frame. What he saw made him fall onto his back, his feet thrust high in the air.

A **proper noun** is a word so specific that it can be applied to only one particular person, place, thing or idea.

common noun: building **proper noun:** The Tower

common noun: animal, terrier, dog **proper noun:** Felix

See page 78 for capitalization rules of proper nouns.

Which nouns in each pair below are common, which proper? Although proper nouns are always capitalized, the proper nouns in this exercise are not. Capitalize them when you write them.

1. city, cleveland
2. girl, susan
3. holiday, halloween
4. mount fuji, mountain
5. military man, colonel sanders
6. sewing machine, singer

Review your understanding of predicates. What action words are needed to make these sentences say something about the subject?

The firecracker high against the night sky.

Virginia the furniture company by check.

A runaway lion footprints in the snow.

Go back to page 13 if you are uncertain about predicates.

Find the predicate in the following sentences. Consider each line a sentence.

1. Sam walked heavily into the truck-stop diner.
2. He leaned on the counter.
3. "I want three burgers, fries and a malt,"
4. he said to Joe, the waiter.
5. Joe jumped right to it.

VERBS COUNT

No words are more important than verbs. They can make your writing strong or weak. Verbs are the heart of the predicate and are the easiest thing to find in a sentence. Finish these two sentences, using only one word for each blank.

Harry Schwarz ＿＿ housework.

Harry Schwarz ＿＿ home in the rain yesterday.

Whatever words you used had to be verbs because no other kind of word would make sense. You might have suggested *loves, hates, likes, abhors* or a similar verb for the first sentence. Your choice for the second sentence was probably *walked* or *came* or *went*, or *skipped*, perhaps. It didn't take much thought for you to put in words that fit and, by doing that, you've shown that you understand how to use two different verb forms: the *-s* form and the *-ed* form.

Most verbs in the English language have these two forms. Look at these subjects and verbs and try to figure out when you use the *-s* form.

I talk   we talk

you talk   you talk

Lee talks   they talk

It's pretty easy to see that only the noun, *Lee*, takes the *-s* form. Since you could substitute *he* or *she, the boy* or *the girl* or even *the horse* for Lee, you can conclude that the *-s* form is used with any single subject except the pronouns *I, you, we* and *they*.

He, she and *it* are called the third person, so the *-s* form is also called the third person singular form. Notice that you don't use the *-s* form with a plural word. You write

Lee talks.   *but*   Lee and Allen talk.

The baby walks.   *but*   The babies walk.

If you can substitute *they* for the subject, it is plural and takes the simple form without -s.

The -*ed* form is also called the past tense form because it shows that something happened in the past.

Yesterday Lee talked.

The winners walked down the street.

There is one other form that verbs take; you probably use it more than any other. Fill in the verb here with two words.

Lee _____ _____ to his sister on the telephone now.

Once again your native sense of English probably guided you to the right words: *is talking*. This is the -*ing* form of the verb. It is always used with a helping verb, and the helping verb is always a form of the verb *be*: *am*, *are* or *is*, *was* or *were*.

As you have seen, verb endings refer to the number of persons performing and the time of the action. These changes are also known as inflections.

Thousands and thousands of verbs in English are formed in a regular pattern from four main or principal parts. These parts are:

1. *watch* **the simple form.** This form is used for all the present verbs except the -*s* form.

2. *watches* The addition of -*es* or -*s* to the simple form creates the **third person singular.**

3. *watched* The addition of -*d* or -*ed* to the simple form creates the **past tense.**

The forms of *be* are listed on page 37.

4. *is watching* The addition of -*ing* forms the **participle.** The participle form is used with the helping verb *be*.

Study the list of regular verbs and their four principal parts.

simple	-s	-ed	-ing
act	acts	acted	acting
add	adds	added	adding
argue	argues	argued	arguing
attack	attacks	attacked	attacking
bathe	bathes	bathed	bathing
bomb	bombs	bombed	bombing

call	calls	called	calling
cry	cries	cried	crying
decay	decays	decayed	decaying
die	dies	died	dying
dine	dines	dined	dining
dive	dives	dived	diving
drown	drowns	drowned	drowning
echo	echoes	echoed	echoing
flow	flows	flowed	flowing
furnish	furnishes	furnished	furnishing
judge	judges	judged	judging
jump	jumps	jumped	jumping
knit	knits	knitted	knitting
knock	knocks	knocked	knocking
linger	lingers	lingered	lingering
measure	measures	measured	measuring
move	moves	moved	moving
notice	notices	noticed	noticing
obey	obeys	obeyed	obeying
occur	occurs	occurred	occurring
offer	offers	offered	offering
perform	performs	performed	performing
pitch	pitches	pitched	pitching
prejudice	prejudices	prejudiced	prejudicing
profit	profits	profited	profiting
sneak	sneaks	sneaked	sneaking
squeal	squeals	squealed	squealing
stay	stays	stayed	staying
stop	stops	stopped	stopping
suppose	supposes	supposed	supposing
tax	taxes	taxed	taxing
try	tries	tried	trying
turn	turns	turned	turning
use	uses	used	using
wrap	wraps	wrapped	wrapping

Select a form for the suggested verbs. Be sure your final sentence makes sense. You may need to refer to the chart for spelling.

use   **1.** I _____ to be afraid of ghosts.

call   **2.** She _____ her mother every day.

add   **3.** You only _____ fuel to the fire when you did that.

move   **4.** We _____ to Denver last year.

suppose	**5.** I _____ that you would do it for her.
cry	**6.** When the baby _____ , feed her.
drown	**7.** They _____ the salad in dressing.
furnish	**8.** That dealer _____ the rods free.
knock	**9.** Someone _____ at the door.
pitch	**10.** He always _____ in for a good cause.
obey	**11.** We only _____ the directions.
attack	**12.** They _____ his argument vigorously.
knit	**13.** Grandma _____ socks for everyone.
try	**14.** Marty _____ to be courteous on the road.
turn	**15.** They always _____ out crooked.
iron	**16.** They always _____ their sheets.
bathe	**17.** He _____ his dog every week.
prejudice	**18.** Books _____ you one way or another.
bomb	**19.** Normally they _____ only military targets.
squeal	**20.** The piglet _____ incessantly.
dine	**21.** He _____ with his mother last night.
wrap	**22.** They _____ packages all night.
echo	**23.** It _____ throughout the glen.
dive	**24.** Marv _____ into the pool without a splash.
jump	**25.** I _____ every time I hear a loud noise.
sneak	**26.** We successfully _____ past the office.
decay	**27.** The onions _____ to a white mush.
hurry	**28.** He _____ home every night.
judge	**29.** Professor Whitley _____ the case.
tax	**30.** The government _____ all imports.
talk	**31.** We sat up and _____ for hours.
notice	**32.** I _____ Mother was limping.

Using the examples as models, do the following.

1. Write five sentences using the -*ing* forms of these verbs. Don't forget to double the final letter.

Example: begin   I think it is *beginning* to rain.

compel	expel	permit	recur
confer	occur	prefer	submit
differ	omit	rebel	transfer

2. Write five sentences using the *-ed* form of these simple forms. Double the final consonant as in the example.

   Example: dip   Marsha *dipped* her cone into the nuts.

fit	rap	shop	stop
knit	sag	skip	strip
knot	ship	step	trip

3. Write five sentences using the *-s* form of the simple verbs here. Remember to change the *y* to *i* before adding the *-es*.

   Example: amplify   His stereo *amplifies* the sound until the room rocks.

carry	deny	fly	rely
cry	dry	marry	reply

4. Write three sentences using the *-s* form of these verbs.

   Example: destroy One serious quarrel *destroys* a relationship.

   display   enjoy   play   relay   decay

5. Write five sentences using the *-ing* form of these verbs. Should the final consonants be doubled?

   Example: exhibit   The artist is *exhibiting* his works tonight.

flavor	kidnap	marvel	pedal
hasten	label	offer	profit

From the chart choose the correct forms to write sentences, using the same verb form as the models. (*See pages* 20-21.)

1. **Example:** argue   *Yesterday he argued against socialized medicine.*
   offer, obey, dine, try, stop, suppose, use, drown, knock, bathe, prejudice

2. *Mary Jane knits sweaters for the Red Cross.*
   drown, dive, attack, argue, squeal, wrap, tax, prejudice, measure

3. *The chipmunk is staying underground for the winter.*
   turn, use, sneak, perform, hurry, jump, dine, cry, attack

4. *The river offers refreshment to the wild animals.*
   stay, turn, use, wrap, bathe, hurry, furnish, flow, echo, drown

5. *Education offers people the opportunity to improve their life style.*
   perform, act, add, attach, move, iron, furnish, use, turn

Using the chart if you need it, supply the correct form of the verb for each sentence below.

Spelling is important!

    The most chilling experience of my life (occur) at a private swimming pool in a resort area. I was (offer) three days' use of it by a friend who (dive) with me every week. While we were (dive), we (argue) about one thing or another. He just (judge) things in a way I do not always understand. To get back to the horror story, I (stay) at his cottage. I wanted to perfect my dive. I (step) out onto the board with some fear. My knees (knock) as I (sneak) to the end of the board. Before I knew it, I (jump). With a smooth flip I (turn) in mid-air and suddenly lost all consciousness. The next thing I (realize), I was at the bottom of the pool. I nearly (drown). How long I (stay) there I don't know, I (suppose) a minute. Then someone (clutch) me around the neck and (drag) me to air and life.

Using the principles you learned from the chart given on pages 20-21, form the following regular verbs correctly. Add -s or -es.

lie
1. He never _____ to me.

issue
2. The Welfare Department _____ food stamps to the needy.

anoint
3. She _____ her sunburned body liberally with lotion.

accept
4. He _____ correction gracefully.

appear
5. Ms. De La Trina _____ in only one number.

tax
6. The government _____ every import barrel.

poison
7. Vassily _____ the rats at the plant.

wish
8. Della _____ for a new routine.

ask
9. Olga _____ the children not to cross through her yard.

drag
10. Oscar _____ his feet.

Add -ed to these simple verbs.

toss
1. She _____ her empty lunchbag into the container.

utter
2. They never _____ a complaint.

play
3. Jim _____ first base.

hail
4. The people _____ Caesar as their king.

desert
5. Finally they _____ the cause.

skate
6. She _____ better than everyone at the rink.

hang
7. They _____ the murderers in the town square.

control
8. Randy _____ the whole market.

profit
9. Danny _____ by your advice.

proceed
10. Vera _____ cautiously in the rain.

Add -*ing* to these simple verbs.

deceive	**1.** I was not ____ you when I told you that.
compel	**2.** She is ____ me to redo this job.
tackle	**3.** Smith was ____ the defensive end.
succeed	**4.** You were ____ until I arrived.
bounce	**5.** The ball was ____ against the plate glass window.
rhyme	**6.** Are you ____ your poem?
transfer	**7.** The family is ____ to Texas.
receive	**8.** Gwen is ____ large checks monthly from her father.
arrive	**9.** They were just ____ when the plane pulled away.
skim	**10.** Forbes is ____ to finish the novel for tomorrow's class.

Complete the following sentences with any form of regular verb. Choose verbs from the lists above or think of your own. Be sure the verb is regular, that is, that it adds -s -ed or -ing to its simple form. Check that the spelling of each is correct.

1. The sunny sky ____ me outdoors.
2. I ____ through the woods; the trees ____ again after a long winter.
3. Tiny green shoots ____ me.
4. Damp earth ____ me everywhere as I ____ through the woods.
5. I ____ that the leaves ____ purple flowers.
6. The purple buds ____ in neat rows one under the other.
7. Droopy green leaves ____ protectively around them.
8. I ____ a strong urge to pick one, but I ____ the groundskeeper heading toward me.
10. Rising I ____ him and ____ on the beautiful weather.

Compose your own sentences using any of the regular verbs. Use the picture for ideas.

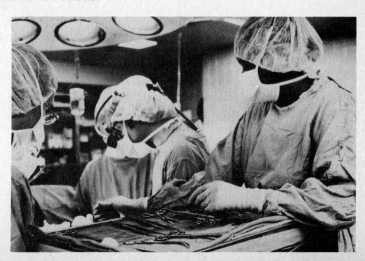

Verbs to Remember

Irregular verbs are something you learned by trial and error. Listen to a young child who is learning to talk. The child has learned how to form the past tense of regular verbs, and applies the rule already learned to other verbs. A toddler learns to say, "I talked to Grandma on the telephone." But when the child says, "The telephone ringed," a parent or older sister or brother corrects him, teaching him to say, "The telephone rang." *Ring* is an irregular verb and every child learns such verbs by making mistakes.

Some irregular verbs never give you trouble. You no longer make the mistake of saying "seed" for "saw," for example, but you may have to stop and think about some others. Do you ever have to ask yourself if it should be "drank" or "drunk"? Or catch yourself wanting to say "costed"? Everybody stumbles over some irregular verbs. Some irregular verbs have no special past tense form. They use the simple form. Here are some examples.

burst	bursts	bursting
cast	casts	casting
cost	costs	costing
cut	cuts	cutting
hit	hits	hitting
hurt	hurts	hurting
put	puts	putting
quit	quits	quitting
read	reads	reading
rid	rids	ridding
set	sets	setting
shed	sheds	shedding
shut	shuts	shutting
slit	slits	slitting
thread	threads	threading
thrust	thrusts	thrusting

Naturally you are tempted to add *-ed* to make the past form as you do for regular verbs. But don't get tripped up by these irregular verbs. Use words from the chart to work out the following sentences.

1. This sweater _____ me ten dollars.
2. He _____ his butter thin.
3. I _____ my job yesterday.
4. She _____ ten books last month.
5. He _____ the carton open with a knife.
6. Marcia _____ a fashionable image at the reception.
7. He _____ his finger on the heart of the problem.

8. The elderly man _____ into tears.

9. It _____ me to see you so depressed.

10. He just _____ his hand through the window.

Make five sentences of your own using any of the verbs.

The other irregular verbs make very noticeable changes in their forms, especially in the past tense. Instead of adding -ed, they change completely.

find   finds   found   finding

go   goes   went   going

begin	begins	began	beginning
blow	blows	blew	blowing
break	breaks	broke	breaking
bring	brings	brought	bringing
catch	catches	caught	catching
choose	chooses	chose	choosing
come	comes	came	coming
do	does	did	doing
drink	drinks	drank	drinking
drive	drives	drove	driving

Supply the past form.

1. At the game we _____ so much soda that we almost exploded.

2. Janet almost _____ old McGregor's window on that last fly.

3. If Felix _____ that coat, that's the one he's got to wear.

4. The constant thumping from the pipes almost _____ me mad.

5. At rush hour the patrolman _____ his whistle in vain.

6. When you _____ the ice cream home, did you put it in the freezer?

7. When the mailman _____ this morning, he _____ good news.

8. Michael _____ his watch again.

9. Randy _____ the assignment while visiting her cousins.

10. I _____ to take lessons six weeks ago.

Write sentences using the past tense of three of the verbs.

eat	eats	ate	eating
fall	falls	fell	falling
fly	flies	flew	flying
freeze	freezes	froze	freezing
get	gets	got	getting
give	gives	gave	giving

go	goes	went	going
hang (picture)	hangs	hung	hanging
know	knows	knew	knowing
lead	leads	led	leading

Supply the past form.

1. Terri just _____ four hot dogs without saying a word.
2. The hound _____ the hunter to the dead pheasant.
3. The ball _____ out into the stands.
4. Gretchen _____ in love with the shivering Chihuahua.
5. Greg _____ the picture over the mantel.
6. I thought he _____ where he was going.
7. Tell me what you _____ for your birthday.
8. The doll _____ a little squeal when you pulled its hair.
9. We almost _____ waiting to get into the ski shelter.
10. Because the brakes were faulty, the car _____ straight into the wall.

Write sentences using the past tense of three of the verbs.

leave	leaves	left	leaving
lie	lies	lay	lying
lose	loses	lost	losing
pay	pays	paid	paying
ride	rides	rode	riding
ring	rings	rang	ringing
rise	rises	rose	rising
run	runs	ran	running
say	says	said	saying
see	sees	saw	seeing

Supply the past form.

1. I thought I just _____ Barbra Streisand in person.
2. The workers _____ the meeting early.
3. Delores _____ a pretty penny for those shoes.
4. The exhausted runaway _____ three hours in a cave.
5. Uncle Tod _____ his grocery store faithfully for thirty years.
6. "Who _____ this horse last?" bellowed the owner.
7. They all stood paralyzed when the phone _____.
8. The sun _____, a ribbon at a time.
9. As a result of the accident, he _____ his driver's license.
10. The weatherman _____ yesterday that it would rain.

Write sentences using the past tense of three of the verbs.

shoot	shoots	shot	shooting
shrink	shrinks	shrank	shrinking
speak	speaks	spoke	speaking
steal	steals	stole	stealing
swing	swings	swung	swinging
take	takes	took	taking
think	thinks	thought	thinking
throw	throws	threw	throwing
wake	wakes	woke	waking
wring	wrings	wrung	wringing
write	writes	wrote	writing

Supply the past form.

1. When I _____ at 8 a.m., I _____ my family a long letter.
2. Tina _____ contentedly on the park swings for half an hour.
3. The sweater stretched out of shape because you _____ it too hard.
4. Besides stretching, it also _____ and is now too small.
5. I _____ you said to meet you at four.
6. He _____ with a Norwegian accent.
7. The player on third _____ a base to bring in the winning run.
8. The worried mother _____ another blanket over the shivering sick child.
9. Teddy _____ an eight-point buck in Pennsylvania.
10. It _____ her all day to get her history done.

Choose a suitable form of the verb for each sentence.

drink   1. She _____ hot coffee every morning.

see   2. I _____ a black limousine approaching me.

steal   3. They _____ secret glances at each other.

lie   4. Yesterday she _____ in the sun three hours.

blow   5. The supervisor _____ the whistle.

lose   6. I know I _____ it in the vicinity.

take   7. Ethel _____ her good old time getting ready.

wring   8. It stretched when I _____ it out.

write   9. She _____ to her sister every week.

rise   10. He _____ hesitantly to his feet.

lead   11. The guide _____ us through the museum.

know   12. He _____ the time had come for farewells.

break   **13.** The waitress _____ a platter.

come   **14.** She _____ twenty minutes early.

give   **15.** Frank _____ us the impression that he's boss.

go   **16.** Last month we _____ to Connecticut.

fly   **17.** The moth _____ straight into the flame.

bring   **18.** I _____ you a refreshing drink.

swing   **19.** They sat and _____ for two hours.

shrink   **20.** The woolen skirt _____ two inches.

Write the right form of the verb for each sentence. If you're not sure of the form, look in the dictionary.

teach   **1.** Angie _____ chemistry for four years.

tell   **2.** Yesterday Don _____ me he's going on vacation.

hide   **3.** The infant _____ the rattle.

sell   **4.** Ask Denny if he _____ his bike yet.

deal   **5.** The cigar-smoking pro _____ the cards expertly.

bleed   **6.** The extortionist _____ his client of all his possessions.

bid   **7.** Moses _____ the Israelites abandon worship of idols.

fling   **8.** The tornado _____ the cottage about like a matchbox.

cling   **9.** The old timer _____ ferociously to his old beliefs.

lend   **10.** The last time I _____ you money, I didn't get it back.

slide   **11.** She _____ all the way down the long hill on her stomach.

sink   **12.** Despite efforts of the Coast Guard, the vessel _____ .

slay   **13.** They believed he _____ four other persons besides.

sit   **14.** The worn doll _____ in the abandoned nursery twenty years.

sing   **15.** Who _____ the solo last year?

string   **16.** She _____ the colorful seeds into an attractive necklace.

win   **17.** The Dolphins _____ the Superbowl several times.

wear   **18.** She accidentally _____ two different shoes.

tear   **19.** When I climbed the crag, I _____ my jeans.

sweep   **20.** The new administration _____ the house clean.

Put the correct form of the listed verbs into the slots.

1. meet   When you __1.__ Mr. Griffin, you __2.__ white. Was
2. become   it because he __3.__ so low in a profound bow, or was

3. bend
4. buy
5. fall
6. flee
7. grind
8. leave
9. begin
10. mean

that when you remembered you __4.__ the wrong ticket? You almost __5.__ over backwards before you __6.__ the scene. I __7.__ my teeth to think you __8.__ before the party really __9.__. I __10.__ no harm in introducing you to him.

Make up your own paragraph using the past tense of any ten verbs you have studied.

The Latest Thing

Take a look at a "Rimed Grammar" from a 1917 textbook. How is it different from the grammar and language lessons you are learning?

Rimed Grammar.—The following anonymous verses will prove an aid to remembering the functions of the parts of speech:

Three little words you often see
Are articles, "a," "an," and "the."

A noun's the name of anything,
As "house" or "garden," "hoop" or "swing."

Instead of nouns the pronouns stand—
"Her" head, "your" face, "his" arm, "my" hand.

Adjectives tell the kind of noun,
As "great," "small," "pretty," "white," or "brown."

A preposition stands before
A noun, as "in" or "through" the door.

Verbs tell of something to be done—
To "sing" or "laugh," "jump," "skip," or "run."

How things are done the adverbs tell,
As "slowly," "quickly," "ill," or "well."

Conjunctions join the words together,
As men "and" women, wind "or" weather.

An interjection shows surprise,
As "'Oh!' How pretty," "'Ah!' How wise."

The whole are called the parts of speech
Which reading, writing, speaking teach.

TWO KINDS OF MODIFIERS

Jack jumped quickly.

How many different ways can you think of to rewrite this sentence as a question?

Who jumped quickly?

What did Jack do?

How did Jack jump? Notice that each question would be answered by a different word from the original sentence: who—Jack, what—jumped, how—quickly. Each word had its own function or answers its own question. The word that answers the question *how* is an adverb. **Adverbs** are a class of words that can be formed in two

If you can't wait to learn about prepositional phrases, turn to page 44.

ways: as single words, *quickly*, or as phrases, *with a smile. Jack jumped with a smile.* One way to recognize adverbs is by their ability to move around. You can put some kinds of adverbs or adverb phrases in several different places in a sentence. Adverbs that tell *how* are especially movable. For example:

> Quickly, Jack jumped.
>
> Jack quickly jumped.
>
> Jack jumped quickly.

The meaning of each sentence is about the same. Only the emphasis is different. Adverbs that tell *how* have another common characteristic: they often (not always!) end in *-ly*.

Find all the "how" adverbs and adverb phrases in these sentences.

1. The rat chewed noisily.
2. The new president graciously bowed to the audience.
3. With a flourish, Mary Louise cut the cake.
4. We gazed hungrily at the campers' bubbling stew.
5. I absolutely refuse to believe that you lied with such a straight face.

Other adverbs answer other questions: *when, where, why* and *to what extent;* adverbs never answer the questions *who* or *what.*

> Jack jumped over the candlestick. (Where did he jump?)
>
> Because of her contrariness, Mary has no friends. (Why doesn't she have friends?)
>
> Bobby Shaftoe left yesterday. (When did he leave?)
>
> I'm terribly worried. (To what extent am I worried?)

Locate the adverb or adverb phrase in each sentence and tell what question it answers, when, where, how, to what extent, why.

1. Bobby Shaftoe has gone to sea.
2. He had silver buckles on his knee.
3. He went by boat.
4. He won't be home until February.
5. His girl friend is very lonesome.
6. Miss Muffet sat on the tuffet.
7. Because of the spider, she left in a hurry.

8. Mary's lamb followed her to school.

9. It walked with a limp.

10. And it baaed loudly outside the classroom.

11. The dish and spoon have run away together!

There is one other form class word (part of speech) you should know. **Adjectives** are describers. They give you more information about a noun or change the meaning of the noun somewhat. Adjectives often come between the determiner and the noun.

the lazy dog
d   adj   n

Besides position, you can recognize adjectives because they also take inflections that are regular. Most adjectives can be inflected to show comparison.

The lazy dog is Fido.

The lazier dog is Rex.

The laziest dog is Toby.

Notice that there is another position for adjectives. You could change these sentences around this way:

You will learn more about this construction on page 38.

Fido is lazy.

Rex is lazier.

Toby is laziest.

Find all the adjectives you can in these sentences.

1. The gray old owl and the striped pussycat went to sea in a beautiful pea-green boat.

2. Spot is such a nasty dog that he chased poor Puff over the high fence.

3. Dick and Jane are good little children.

4. Roger, however, is unkind.

5. Where are you going, my pretty young maid?

You remember a number of nursery rhymes and children's stories. Let your imagination go. Use adjectives to create vivid scenes and characters from those stories. Describe sights, sounds, tastes, smells, touches and other qualities.

Jack Horner   Hey Diddle Diddle   Jack Sprat
Billy Goats Gruff   Three Little Pigs   Peter Pumpkin Eater

STRUCTURES

A brownstone, a villa, an historic monument—three kinds of structures with the same purpose—to provide shelter. Language, too, has many different kinds of structures with one purpose—to communicate.

The sentence structure you examined earlier is the simple sentence—one subject and one predicate. As you know, the noun is the main word of the subject, and the verb is the key word in the predicate. Subjects are fairly standard; they consist of either nouns and their modifiers (determiners and adjectives) or pronouns. But predicates are a little more complex. There are several kinds of predicates; in order to recognize the different kinds, you have to be familiar with a few different kinds of verbs.

Transitive verbs are verbs that pass action from the doer to the receiver. The subject is the doer. Words that receive the action are **objects.** They answer the question *what* or *whom.*

1. The quarterback passed the ball.
   What did the quarterback pass?

2. Paul struck his brother.
   Whom did Paul strike?

The direct objects are 1. the ball and 2. his brother. Just like subjects, direct objects are either nouns and their modifiers or pronouns. The difference is that the object is receiving the action.

Identify the direct object in each of the following sentences.

1. Mike whistled a tune.
2. Jennie loudly whistled a tune.
3. Mike whistled a tune loudly.
4. Earl saved the girl from drowning.
5. Gigi saw the mosquito on the ceiling.
6. At halftime, Kathy waved her baton expertly.
7. The dog dug a hole for its bone.
8. Allison hung the curtains on the rod.
9. Hazel hung an original painting over her sofa.
10. Loyalty drove the men to heroism.

Write sentences that contain at least one direct object using the following verbs.

called	read
whispered	startled
studied	soothed
purchases	stretched
delivered	bathed

In these two sentences, which verb does not have a direct object?

The monkey danced.

Kathleen grows plants.

You can easily see that the first sentence is complete after the verb, danced. Verbs that do not direct action toward an object are called **intransitive.** Such verbs do not need an object to make the sentence complete.

The prefix *in-* changes the meaning of *transitive* to a negative.

The robin chirped.

Our neighbor moved.

Even if other words follow the verb, unless they receive the action, the verb is intransitive.

The robin chirped noisily. (How—not what)

Our neighbor moved to Dallas. (Where)

You should recognize *noisily, out loud,* and *to Dallas* as adverbs.
Some verbs can be transitive or intransitive. You must look for an object in order to decide which kind of verb you see. Notice how the same verbs can take objects.

The robin chirped its morning song. (What did it chirp?)

Our neighbor moved her potted palm. (What did she move?)

Some of the sentences below contain no object. The verbs are intransitive. Others take an object. Those verbs are transitive. Find the verb in each sentence. If the verb has no object, label it as the dictionary does, *vi*. If it has an object, write the object and label the verb *vt*.

1. The annual speech contest stirs a great deal of activity.
2. Students practice for weeks ahead.
3. They polish their speeches and their delivery.
4. Their teachers coach them daily.
5. Contest officials choose experts in public speaking to judge.
6. The day arrives.
7. Everyone is nervous except the judges.
8. Some perform with ease.
9. Others quake and tremble.
10. Finally the officials choose the top speakers in the area.

The third important kind of verb is called a **linking verb.** It acts like a link in a chain. What two nouns are linked in this sentence?

Alfredo is my brother.

Sometimes linking verbs are compared to equal signs because they show the same relationship. Alfredo *equals* my brother.
The main linking verb is *be* and all the forms of *be*. The forms are:

Do not confuse the verb *be* and the auxiliary *be* (page 20). Think of them as two different words.

(I) am, was, have been (we) are, were, have been
(you) are, were, have been (you) are, were, have been
(he, she, it) is, was, has been (they) are, were, have been

Be and its forms can link the subject with a

or

noun: Miss Muffet is a sissy.

adjective: Miss Muffet is timid.

Be can also be followed by an

adverb: Miss Muffet is here.

Find the linking verb in each sentence. Tell whether the word after the linking verb is a noun, adjective or adverb.

1. Father is overweight.
2. The crayon is broken.
3. The child is a boy.
4. A banana peel is slippery.
5. A banana is a fruit.
6. Tomatoes are cheap this season.
7. My records are finally here!
8. Bread is nourishing.
9. His breakfast was all liquids.
10. Linda's Pekinese was always trembling.
11. Mr. Quigley has been sick for three days.
12. Beverly Adams has been office manager for two years.
13. In her childhood, old Mrs. Simms had been sickly.
14. Strawberries were cheap last month.
15. Linking verbs are easy to identify.
16. You should have been at the play.
17. Is it already nine o'clock?
18. Those shoes might be too tight.
19. Could this be the end of class already?
20. To think I might have been a great opera star!

Write three sentences, using a linking verb in each. In the first sentence, follow the verb with a noun; in the second, an adjective; in the third, an adverb.

A few other verbs besides *be* can be used as linking verbs.

(*was*)
She appeared sick.

(*am*)
I feel dizzy.

(*was*)
He remained captain until the end.

(*is*)
The music sounds flat.

Some other linking verbs are:

become He *becomes* melancholy on Sunday.

feel Iris *feels* tired.

get The baby *got* sick again.

look You *look* awful.

remain The dog *remained* faithful.

seem Archer *seems* nervous.

smell The milk *smells* sour.

taste These oranges *taste* sweet.

Notice that in each case a form of *be* can be substituted for these linking verbs.

See page 15 for ways to identify nouns; page 33 will help you with adjectives.

You can automatically tell that a verb is not a linking verb if the noun or pronoun following it is not equal to it.

Make exciting sentences by using any ten of the linking verbs listed. Remember to follow them with nouns and adjectives that are equal to them. Write the form of *be* that can substitute for the linking verb above it in a parenthesis.

(is)
Example: looks That hat *looks* ridiculous on you.

Identify the linking verbs below. Tell whether the word after the verb is a noun or an adjective.

1. Gemma is the third person I've seen with a red scarf.
2. Doctor Gemlatch seems elated about the operation.
3. Gail kicked the ball a phenomenal distance.
4. Do you think Bruce is better at math?
5. The nation appears economically stable.
6. The children were contented with their crayon books.
7. Jacqueline was sure of her ability to win the match.
8. Great-grandfather once was a personal servant of a general.
9. The convoy was capable of stopping the enemy.
10. Your bill is thirty dollars.

Substitute a linking verb for the equal sign in these sentences. Choose a form of *be* or another linking verb that fits the time and number (singular or plural) of the sentence.

1. Pete = sick.
2. The dog = black and white.
3. I = an American.
4. You = a doctor.
5. Last summer he = a lifeguard at the pool.
6. Last night they = happy about the performance.
7. The doughnuts = greasy this morning.
8. She = proud of your show.
9. I = not the one you are looking for.
10. Stanley = the winner.

Write a sentence for each picture here using the linking verbs *sound*, *feel*, *smell* and *look*. Then write a second sentence with the same verbs as nonlinking verbs.

Working Together

Here's an easy matching quiz.

Some people have trouble getting the subject and the predicate of a sentence to agree, but subject and verb agreement can be easy if you realize that there is only one problem—getting the numbers to match.

The **number** of a word shows whether it refers to one person or thing or idea or to more than one. When a word refers to one person, thing or idea, it is singular in number. When it refers to two or more, it is plural.

If you have trouble, turn back to page 16.

Tell whether the following words are singular or plural. If you cannot tell from the form here, write *either*.

1. person	11. any
2. churches	12. jury
3. three	13. members
4. Patricia	14. women
5. gas	15. neither
6. he	16. Roy and Al
7. deer	17. secretary-treasurer
8. mothers-in-law	18. measles
9. metropolis	19. everyone
10. every	20. these

You know that most nouns form their plural by adding -s or -es. Verbs, too, have singular and plural forms. The third person singular, or -s form, is the only form that can be a problem. All pronouns except *he, she,* and *it* take the simple form. Singular nouns also take the -s form.

Not sure about verb forms? Go back to page 20.

Read each word group below. Write C if the forms in the group match in number. Write X if they don't.

1. He trots	11. That pianist sing
2. She skip	12. His mother think
3. Dan do	13. Her gerbil leave
4. The bug jumps	14. The baby sleeps
5. Mickey lies	15. A book fall
6. The radio work	16. She do
7. It taste	17. The fireman throws
8. The piano were	18. It does
9. A tomato drops	19. The player pass
10. They looks	20. The coffee remains

A verb agrees with its subject-noun in number. Singular subjects take singular verbs.

The *cow chews* her cud all day.
Cow *is singular. Chews is third person singular.*

The *squirrel* in our park *eats* out of my hand.
Squirrel *is singular. Eats is third person singular.*

Plural subjects take plural verbs.

The *cows chew* their cud all day.

Cows *is plural.* Chew *is plural.*

The *squirrels* in our park *eat* out of my hand.

Squirrels *is plural.* Eat *is plural.*

Hint: Use only one *-s* at a time. If the subject ends in *-s,* the predicate does **not.**

Supply the correct verb form for the following subjects. Remember that only third person singular takes *-s.* **Don't use the past tense.**

sing   **1.** Monica _____ well.

sing   **2.** I _____ loudly.

sing   **3.** They _____ together as a group.

dance   **4.** We _____ every Friday night.

cook   **5.** You _____ the most luscious meals.

like   **6.** Horses _____ cubes of sugar.

prefer   **7.** She _____ lemon meringue to apple pie.

do   **8.** He _____ not want his name known.

be   **9.** That pattern _____ too small for you.

be   **10.** We _____ certain of a victory.

Choose the *-s* **form or the simple form.**

need   **1.** The pictures on the wall _____ straightening.

require **2.** Her demands for delivery _____ immediate attention.

file   **3.** Barbara _____ her accident claim today.

be   **4.** Sentimentality in films _____ going out of style.

be   **5.** Paying taxes _____ not the only way to be a good citizen.

frighten **6.** Frankenstein _____ little children.

turn   **7.** In winter the leaves _____ a rich gold.

have   **8.** _____ the doctor made his rounds yet?

do   **9.** _____ the board meet tonight?

include **10.** This recording _____ four songs.

Supply the form that will make sense.

have   **1.** Do you _____ your tax return form in yet?

         2. My brother _____ but I _____ not.

be   **3.** What _____ you waiting for?

do   **4.** My CPA _____ not have any more forms.

be   **5.** Here _____ some of mine.

have **6.** Thanks. You _____ been a help.

be   **7.** I _____ glad to be of service.

have **8.** It _____ been a long time since I met anyone so helpful.

do   **9.** _____ not mention it.

be   **10.** _____ you kidding?

PHRASEMAKERS

You met these phrases on page 32.

You have worked with adverb phrases such as these:

> to the store (where)
>
> with a smile (how).

These phrases are considered adverbs because they work the same way a one-word adverb does. You can see that there are two or three words in the phrase, and you should be able to spot the determiner and noun:

> the   store
> **d**   **n**
> a   smile

The other word in the phrase is a **preposition.** Prepositions have only one use — to join the phrase to the rest of the sentence. Not all prepositional phrases are adverbs; some work like adjectives.

> The man in the blue suit is a policeman.

In this case, *in the blue suit* is an adjective phrase because it modifies *the man.* You should learn to recognize prepositional phrases easily, because they sometimes interfere with subject-verb agreement. You can recognize them by their regular structure

The mathematical symbol ± tells you that the article and adjective are optional.

> preposition ± article ± adjective + noun or pronoun

Although the phrases may or may not have articles and adjectives, they will always have a preposition and a noun or pronoun.

> Reggie went *to bed.* (preposition + noun)
>
> Patty Cake lives *at the zoo.* (preposition + article + noun)
>
> I walked *down the slippery road.* (preposition + article + adjective + noun)

Prepositions themselves are a fixed class of words; there are fewer than fifty in English. You should memorize them so you can recognize them. Here are some common prepositions.

about	before	except	on
above	behind	for	over
across	below	from	through
after	beside	in	to
against	between	inside	toward
among	by	into	under
around	down	of	up
at	during	off	with

Find the prepositional phrases in this paragraph.

In winter I sometimes get depressed. I think about taking trips to Florida or sailing around the world on a banana boat. I suppose it seems silly to you, but, at time, I just get tired of studying. Between December and April, I am up to my ears in papers, and I feel like I could crawl into bed and stay there for months.

Loners and Mixers

Certain pronouns dictate whether verbs will be singular or plural. The following pronouns are always singular.

each	anyone	no one
either	everyone	someone
one	anybody	nobody
neither	everybody	somebody

Each of the girls *is* allowed three minutes.

Everyone has a box lunch.

Has anybody in the room reported the fire?

Notice that these pronouns are often followed by a prepositional phrase. Make the verb agree with the pronoun subject, not with the noun in the prepositional phrase.

The following pronouns are plural: *both, few, many, several.*

A *few* of this breed of mosquito *are* dangerous.

Several want to take their own dinner along.

The pronouns *some, all, most, any* and *none* can be singular or plural. *Some, all* and *most* are singular when they refer to quantity and plural when they refer to separate items.

Some of the ammunition *was* housed in the arsenal.

Some of the guns *were* kept in the barracks.

All the staff *was* happy with the votes.

All the teachers *were* pleased with the decision.

Most of the flour *was* gone.

Most of the flowers *were* picked over.

Any and *none* are singular if each item is thought of individually and plural if items are thought of as a group.

Any of the oranges *passes* the test. (any single one)

Any of the oranges *pass* the test. (all the oranges)

None of the schools *was* suitable. (not any single school)

None of the schools *were* open. (no schools)

If there is a prepositional phrase, try reading the sentence without it.

Choose the right verb for the following sentences.

1. (Does, Do) either of the dogs have a white-tipped tail?
2. Some of the voters (want, wants) Nell to be president.
3. One of the men (is, are) going to Toronto.
4. Everybody in the school (likes, like) the cafeteria's food.
5. Naturally all of the cake (was, were) eaten.
6. All the cookies (was, were) gone too.
7. Neither of the children (do, does) any housework.
8. All the boys (pitch, pitches) in to help.
9. Both his manuscripts (was, were) rejected.
10. Some of the cleanser always (remain, remains) in the tub.

seem   1. Mary _____ to catch cold easily.

have   2. Is there a cure? None _____ been discovered as yet.

have   3. Several _____ been tried, however.

have   4. Of the twenty-five tested, none _____ succeeded completely.

become 5. A few people _____ slightly better after an injection.

1. Somebody on the ski slopes (is, are) doing some fancy stunts.
2. (Do, Does) each employee get a free turkey?
3. Most of the trash (gets, get) burned in our incinerator.
4. Would you believe nobody (is, are) exempt?
5. Any of the juices (has, have) vitamin C.
6. Either of the belts (go, goes) with this outfit.
7. None of the stations (has, have) anything good on tonight.
8. We'll be lucky if someone (volunteer, volunteers).
9. (Does, Do) anybody want to take the job?
10. Nobody (begin, begins) before the gun.

Does is a form of the irregular verb *do*. See page 27.

Doesn't is a contraction for *does not*.

Don doesn't swim. She doesn't like sweets.

Don't is a contraction for *do not*.

I *don't* like potato chips.

You *don't* look well in green.

Write the correct verb, *don't* or *doesn't*.

1. I _____ dive since I hurt my back.
2. You _____ want me to help, do you?
3. The singers _____ tour anymore.
4. He _____ particularly enjoy hamburgers.
5. Maureen _____ have green eyes.
6. Cats _____ have brown eyes, do they?
7. She _____ care what she puts in her soup.
8. Morris _____ like dog food.
9. These dishes _____ break very easily.
10. This dish _____ belong to the set.

Write sentences using any of the subjects in the first two columns and adding *don't* or *doesn't* to any of the verbs in the last two columns.

The senators	He	know	have
Bella	She	hate	know
A pen	It	cost	feel
The scarf	They	love	need
Spaghetti	We	keep	sing
A new camera	You	thrill	light
Trains	Dictionaries	capture	go
The dance		rule	

Review

enjoy   **1.** I _____ good TV films.

have   **2.** They _____ to be true portrayals of life.

do   **3.** I can't stand those that _____ n't have an exciting plot.

do   **4.** But Steve _____ n't mind if the plot is thin.

be   **5.** All my friends _____ also particular about the films they watch.

is   **6.** The news _____ of top interest to them, then documentaries.

prefer   **7.** But none _____ the news to an A-1 film.

be   **8.** Andy and Martha _____ the exception. They like news better.

be   **9.** When the mumps _____ going around, we watched TV all day.

be   **10.** Several of the soap operas _____ a waste of time.

move   **11.** The plot _____ at a snail's pace.

take   **12.** It _____ five days to perform a simple action.

refuse   **13.** Both of my children _____ to watch soap operas.

do   **14.** Maribeth _____ not object to the children's programs, though.

watch   **15.** I suspect many children _____ Sesame Street.

do   **16.** All the children I know _____ .

help   **17.** That kind of show _____ children in school, they say.

be   **18.** I _____ not sure it _____ really helpful to them.

watch   **19.** If anybody _____ TV too much, he or she becomes passive.

need   **20.** But everyone _____ a little entertainment in his life.

be   **21.** Someone in the group _____ responsible.

want   **22.** No one _____ the scholarship.

get   **23.** Every dog in the kennel _____ the finest food.

do   **24.** Either of the twins _____ the job well.

be   **25.** Each of the windows _____ cracked.

like   **26.** Neither of the children _____ farina.

You should be familiar with this symbol and its meaning. It is a symbol for the word "and"; companies often use it in their names, Doubleday & Company. The symbol has a name which you probably don't know: ampersand. Ampersand is a shortened version of the longer expression "and per se and." Unless you're taking notes for yourself, or designing a business card, you don't use the ampersand. It is too informal for your papers. But you probably use the word *and* frequently. You use it to join two equal elements, in a compound subject, for example.

Two or more subject nouns joined by *and* form a compound subject.

> **simple subject:**   Jim went to the store.
>
> **compound subject:**   Jim and Kath went to the store.
>
> **compound subject:**   Jim, Kath and Mike went to the store.

Predicates, too, can be compound when two or more verbs are joined by *and*.

> **simple predicate:**   Jim got up.
>
> **compound predicate:**   Jim got up and ate breakfast.
>
> **compound predicate:**   Jim got up, dressed and ate breakfast.

Remember that although the elements (subject and predicate) may be compound, you still have only a simple sentence, one compound subject and/or one compound predicate.

Find the compounds in these simple sentences.

1. Suspecting nothing, Kenneth and Mel turned the corner.
2. To their surprise, they saw two men climbing into a basement window.
3. The burglar turned, spotted them and ran.
4. Ken and Mel gave the would-be criminal a terrible chase.
5. Finally they gave up and turned toward home.

Construct a sentence with both a compound subject and a compound predicate.

Compound subjects and predicates can be joined by some other conjunctions, especially *or* and *nor*. Or can be used alone or with *either; nor* is usually used with *neither*.

Compound Subjects:

Rice or macaroni goes well with tomato sauce.

Either Ethel or André serves table eight.

Neither sherbet nor pudding would please you tonight.

Compound Predicates:

I *neither looked at nor saw* your lost book.

You *either cry or laugh*.

At the meetings we *sit or stand*.

Find the compounds in these simple sentences.

1. Curtains or drapes will be put up later.
2. The baby fusses or screams all day long.
3. Neither paint nor wallpaper would be appropriate.
4. Fish or cut bait!
5. I will either go to college or join the navy.
6. Neither Mary nor Margaret is home yet.
7. They are either clever or lucky.

Couples

Compound subjects joined by *and* take plural verbs.

Arnold *and* Melissa *believe* in socialized medicine.

Both people believe. Notice that even though each subject is singular, the two together joined by *and* take a plural verb. Of course plural subjects joined by *and* take a plural verb.

Leaves *and* flowers *suffer* at winter's approach.

Singular subjects joined by *or* or *nor* take a singular verb.

Ron *or* Gerri *gets* up for the 2 a.m. feeding every night.

Either one gets up.

Neither a note *nor* a signature *holds* up in court.

Neither one holds up.

Supply the needed verb.

The forms of *be* are on page 37.

be   **1.** Your gloves and purse _____ still in the car.

be   **2.** Your hat or purse _____ found on the bus.

be   **3.** A new car and a three-week vacation _____ my idea of prizes.

be   **4.** Spaghetti and chicken cacciatore _____ his favorite dishes.

take off **5.** Every month David or Therese _____ for a three-day business trip.

do   **6.** Will and Pete _____ not take their work seriously.

be   **7.** Will or Pete _____ always complaining.

begin   **8.** Third or fourth quarter, I'm not sure which, _____ tomorrow.

be   **9.** A flashbulb or flashcube _____ important for indoor shots.

be   **10.** Cartridges or rolls _____ expensive.

Write the singular or plural verb to be used in each sentence.

be   **1.** Exxon or General Motors _____ usually the biggest corporation.

be   **2.** Sears, Roebuck, Safeway Stores, and K Mart _____ among the largest companies in the U.S.

produce **3.** South Africa and Canada _____ the most gold.

have   **4.** Compared with other monetary bills, through the years, $5,000 or $10,000 bills _____ the least numbers in circulation.

lead	**5.** Texas and Iowa _____ the U.S. in cattle raising.
sell	**6.** General Motors and Ford _____ the largest number of passenger cars.
be	**7.** Gas or oil _____ the second greatest source of electrical energy in the U.S.
be	**8.** Either Ohio or Indiana _____ second to Pennsylvania in steel production.
pay	**9.** General Motors and Ford Motor Company _____ their top executives high salaries annually.
do	**10.** From the number of telephones in each city, New York and Los Angeles _____ the most calling.

If you have trouble, go back to page 13.

Refresh your memory by dividing these sentences into two parts, subject and predicate. Remember that the subject is the noun and all its modifiers, and the predicate is the verb with its completers and modifiers.

1. The baby took her first step today.
2. With a little glue, she repaired the broken vase.
3. A musty and soiled washcloth hung over the greasy sink.
4. Miss Bumbry sang the aria with perfect ease.
5. The withered and arthritic old man sneezed painfully.
6. Sirius is the brightest star in Orion.
7. A parsec is equal to 3.26 light years.
8. White dwarfs are about one million times denser than the sun.
9. The bride tripped on the step and sprawled before the minister.
10. Her horrified groom and the nervous best man laughed helplessly.

FRAGMENTS AND RUN-ONS

By now you should be an expert at identifying the two basic elements of the sentence—subject and predicate. In writing, every sentence must be complete; it must have a subject and a predicate. Sometimes in informal situations, you speak in phrases or in parts of sentences, especially in reply to a question:

"Hi, Jill. Where are you going?" "Downtown."

The single word "downtown" is enough to answer the question, but it isn't a complete sentence. However, such sentence pieces are not allowed in writing.

If you have a paper returned with the comment *frag*, you are not writing complete sentences. A "frag" or **sentence fragment** is part of a sentence, not a complete sentence.

I like most fruits for breakfast. Except prunes.

You can easily see that "except prunes" has no verb; therefore, it is a sentence fragment.

Many fragments are phrases like "except prunes" which can simply be added to the sentence before or after it. Remember that a long word group is not a sentence unless it has a subject and a predicate.

Find the fragments in the following exercise and add them to the complete sentence at an appropriate place. Underline the part that was once a fragment.

> **Example:** I like most fruits for breakfast, <u>except prunes.</u>

1. If you love horses, you can be a trainer. Or a vet.
2. Or you can ride until you're good enough to jump. Like other prize-winning equestrians.
3. Plenty of experience and time in the saddle is important. And a good coach.
4. You have to take riding seriously. To spend three hours every day in the saddle.
5. You've got to work up a positive relationship with your horse who must respond to you completely. But not sense your nervousness.

Don't be confused by phrases that begin with an -*ing* word.

> Looking under her bed for her shoes. Jane bumped her head.

See page 20.

Although *looking* is the participle form of the verb, it is not really a verb unless it has the helping verb *be*. And, you can see that there is no subject. The easiest way to correct this fragment problem is to attach the fragment to the sentence either at the beginning or the end.

> Looking under her bed for her shoes, Jane bumped her head.

> Jane bumped her head looking under her bed for her shoes.

Rewrite these sentences, correcting fragments by incorporating them into the sentence.

1. Listening to the radio every morning and evening. The lonely child found some recreation.
2. Starting up the ignition with a grunt, snort and scrape. Phil rubbed his leather gloves together with satisfaction.

3. Freezing the ice cream and keeping it frozen. This was the challenge of the busy ice cream stand.

4. He drove all the neighbors wild. Practicing almost incessantly on the drum for three months.

5. Settling for a scrap of food and a dirty coat. The beggar turned away disappointed.

Make up your own sentences to incorporate the following fragments either at the beginning or end.

1. very early in the morning
2. ending the race with a cry of victory
3. but not alone at midnight
4. finally looking up the word in the dictionary
5. to accept the criticism of friends and relatives
6. begging his friend's forgiveness
7. fortunately not her collection of **paintings**.
8. hanging drapes at the end of the day
9. in the cellar under the steps
10. building as good a fire as any boy scout

More on sentence punctuation on page 89.

In each group below there are two word groups that are punctuated as sentences. Identify the real sentences as *S* and the fragments as *F*. Then correct the error by building complete sentences. You may add, change or take out words.

1. Dogs and cats should engage in several activities. A little running, a little playing, a little hunting and a little sleeping.

2. But eating. That's the most enjoyable activity of all.

3. You have to consider three things. Nutrition, appetite and your budget.

4. Coming in three basic types. Complete cat and dog foods are available in dry, semi-moist and moist form.

5. Sold in bags from one to fifty pounds. Dog food is least expensive.

6. The middle price range is composed of one-serving packets. Of semi-moist consistency.

7. Finally, the canned foods. They are most expensive.

8. Reward your pet now and then. With special treat foods in cans or biscuits.

9. Some dogs stay on one food they're trained to. For life.

10. Turning up their noses and rejecting what you've fed them for years. Cats are more unpredictable.

11. Almost everyone was rescued from the burning house. All but Peterson.

12. Not a cent. Not one red cent will I leave to that no-good grandson.

13. Stealing noiselessly into the house. He was surprised to find his father at the top of the stairs.

14. Houses in California are made of sturdy materials. Such as concrete and stucco.

15. Following the dog's muddy tracks, they found him. Cowering in a corner, aware of his misdeeds.

Rewrite the following paragraphs correcting any fragments. Check that each sentence has its own subject and predicate.

1. You'll enjoy shopping by mail. You can see all the items available. At a glance. You can take your good old time. Making a decision. And best of all. The mailman is the only one who will end up with sore feet.

2. But there are some disadvantages. To mail order or phone shopping. You can't actually see the product. You may choose something unfit. Not as glamorous as on the ad page. Then too, it isn't always wise to send money ahead, especially to unfamiliar mail order companies.

3. When you do order something by mail. Identify your order. Completely. This may sound silly, but some people forget important information. Like their name and address. Keep a copy of your order. Together with the name and address of the company. And the date. Paying by money order or check and including tax, shipping and postage costs. You'll save yourself a lot of headaches.

Double-Deckers

Compound elements are on page 49.

You have learned about compound elements within a simple sentence. Now you are ready to join two related sentences. It can be done. The easiest way is to connect two complete sentences by one of these six conjunctions preceded by a comma.

Subject and predicate , AND subject and predicate.

, BUT

, OR

, FOR (when it means *because*)

, YET

I went shopping, AND Milly went skating.

Each complete sentence legally joined into one sentence is called a **clause**. The new double-decker is a **compound sentence**.

Frances likes ice cream , BUT Alma prefers steak.

Notice that when *for* is used as a preposition, the words that follow it do not contain a subject and predicate and so the sentence is not compound.

Marguerite stepped down, FOR she had just become top medalist.

Brenda bought a pair of earrings FOR her mother.

Take another look at page 45 to review prepositional phrases.

Make the following into legitimate compound sentences. Remember that a comma is not enough to separate two independent clauses unless they are very, very short. Your job will be to replace the first period with a comma, add one of the six conjunctions and remove the capital beginning the second sentence.

Wrong   I saved for a red plaid shirt, he spent his money on food.

Right   I saved for a red plaid shirt, but he spent his money on food.

1. Some people tend to be "day" people. They easily snap to it before sunrise.
2. Early birds are often finished after dinner or near four. They don't wake up again till sunrise.
3. Others find it hard to rise. They do not find it easy to be cheerful till after dinner.
4. They are the life of the party beginning at five in the afternoon. They are still raring to go at two in the morning.
5. Some people include a bit of both. They may have two low and two high points a day.
6. Plants and animals are equipped with biological calendars. Humans are too.
7. Daily cycles ebb and flow in rhythms. Body temperature, blood pressure, blood sugar, breathing and pulse rate vary around a day.
8. These rhythms operate on a rough cycle of 24 hours. They are probably inherited.
9. The story of human rhythms is a new field. There have always been people who understood the human time sense.
10. People cannot expect to do their best work when body temperature is at its lowest. They cannot expect to sleep when body temperature is highest.

Tell whether the following are true compound sentences. Remember a compound sentence has two independent clauses, each with its own subject and predicate. Some of the sentences may have compound subjects or predicates.

1. The chimney was blocked, and we had smoke all through the house.
2. According to the weatherman, it is going to rain all day.
3. I like rain, but Roger doesn't.
4. The house across the street has disappeared in the fog and rain.
5. Fog brings a pleasant quiet, but it can be dangerous for the driver.
6. The dull granite and white marble of the cathedral are spotted with rain.
7. I have a terrible stomach ache and cannot come with you.
8. Sarah Jane has left a bowl of milk for yet another stray cat.
9. The landlord will lower the rent, or we will move.
10. Compound subjects and compound predicates are not difficult to recognize.

Write three original compound sentences. Remember that the comma goes before the conjunction, not after.

Weak Links

Sometimes people forget that two clauses can only be joined by one of the six conjunctions preceded by a comma. They think they can hold them together by a comma alone. This error is known as a *comma fault* or *run-on sentence*.

Rewrite the following paragraphs and correct the comma faults and fragments. In some cases the comma in a legitimate compound sentence has been misplaced. Put it in the right place.

Example: Save yourself some money, there is a sale at Merthe's.

Save yourself some money, for there is a sale at Merthe's.

1. You can cover 350 square feet of wall or ceiling with a gallon of paint. First you'll need to cover floors and furniture with drop cloths, you can buy inexpensive pieces of plastic or you can use old sheets or large pieces of canvas. Next you should remove all light switch and wall plug plates, then you should cover baseboards, and window frame edges with masking tape. Filling in plastic cracks and holes with spackling compound is the next step, when it is dry you can sand it smooth.

2.   Like people, paint prefers weather that is in-between, not too hot and not too cold, rainy days are also bad. To prevent splattering and dripping. You should dip your brush into the paint only one third the length of the bristles. The order is woodwork first. Ceiling next. Finally the walls. You can begin at the upper left hand corner of a wall. Working toward the floor in a narrow strip. Painting two-foot strips just below the ceiling line is the next step, then you can finish the wall.

3. At the baseboard. You can use a brush for areas the roller couldn't reach. You'll want to wipe up spills and splatters or drips immediately, it is harder to get dry paint off. Above all at the end. You will save paint and brushes. By tightly replacing the lid on the paint can and, cleaning brushes and roller. To save money. You should know that paint looks deeper and darker on a wall than on the sample color card.

Write an original composition on "how to do" something you are an expert at. When you have finished the first draft, go over your work with a magnifying glass to find any tack-ons, *-ing* openers or other fragments. Get rid of comma faults and run-ons. Submit a paper where every sentence makes sense.

Above exercise adapted by permission from Co-Ed, © 1975 by Scholastic Magazines, Inc.

Exercise on page 56 adapted by permission from Forecast, © 1975 by Scholastic Magazines, Inc.

Sound-Alikes

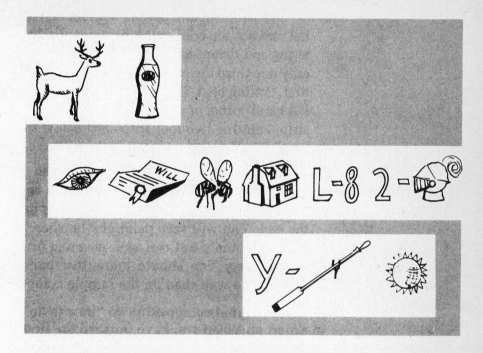

This is an example of a rebus, a message written in a picture code. Can you decode the message? Rebuses are built on homonyms or words that sound alike. What homonyms can you think of for *deer, eye, bee* and *sun*?

Homonyms can be a sticky problem in writing. In speaking, if you know how to pronounce a word and use it meaningfully, you have no problem. But in writing, you not only have to know the sound and meaning, you have to know the correct spelling to be sure you get the right meaning across.

Study each group of words; then choose the word that fits the context in the exercise following each group.

Group One

allowed	No one is *allowed* to use this door. (Think *allow.*)
aloud	He prayed *aloud.* (Think *loud.*)
ate	The hungry man couldn't remember when he last *ate.*
eight	If we add your four eggs to my *eight,* we'll have an even dozen.

bare   Rex chewed the meat down to the *bare* bone.

bear   The *bear* caught the peanuts in his mouth.
Can you *bear* the pain without novocain?

blew   The Pied Piper *blew* his horn.

blue   Africa is the land of *blue* skies.

brakes His *brakes* squealed as he jolted to a halt.

breaks Marti always *breaks* the best china.
He's had some lucky *breaks*.

1. Why didn't you apply your (brakes, breaks) earlier?
2. The (blew, blue) sky distracted me.
3. Then by the time I (blew, blue) my horn, we'd crashed.
4. Are you insured? Yes, but I'm not (allowed, aloud) to claim the first $250.
5. That will leave my wallet (bear, bare).
6. Those are the (brakes, breaks).
7. I'm not sure I can (bear, bare) it.

Write one original sentence for each word you didn't use.

Group Two

board   I'll need another *board* for this platform.

bored   Ellen is *bored* with her job.

buy   What can you *buy* for three dollars? (Think, *U buy*.)

by   The book was illustrated *by* George Graham.
They went *by* the house. I'll see you *by* and *by*.

cell   A *cell* divides by mitosis.

sell   How many candle holders did you *sell*?

cent   The state tax went up one *cent*.

scent   The hounds lost the *scent* at the river.

sent   I *sent* the letter yesterday.

coarse The beggar slept under a *coarse* blanket.

course Of *course* I'm coming.
The golf *course* needed mowing.
What *courses* are you taking this year?

canvas   The *canvas* tents flapped in the wind.

canvass   The heart fund will *canvass* this area for contributions. (Think, extra *s* for extra work.)

We went (by, buy) the (canvas, canvass) and (board, bored) booth where they had exotic perfumes to (cell, sell). Of (coarse, course) the (cent, scent) drew us to (buy, by) at least one sample. Some (coarse, course) persons jarred me just as I opened my purse and (cent, sent, scent) the coins rolling on the ground. I had to (canvas, canvass) the entire area before I recovered the final (scent, cent, sent).

Write one original sentence for each word you didn't use.

Group Three

dear   She lost a *dear* friend when Emily moved.

deer   The *deer* had one broken antler.

desert   Do not *desert* the ideals of your youth. (verb)
The trip across the *desert* dehydrated the baby. (noun)

dessert   Lemon meringue pie was his favorite *dessert*.

fair   She was *fair*, though her sister was dark.
The *fair* opens tomorrow.
He has a *fair* chance of getting into college.
It's just not *fair* to expect to eat without working.

fare   The bus *fare* was fifty dollars round trip.

flour   The bag of *flour* was infested with weevils.

flower   A single *flower* can touch a cold heart.

for   *For* the third time, it's time to get up.

fore   "*Fore!*" shouted the golfer as his ball headed for the green.

four   Is *four* dollars too much for gloves?

Although the (fare, fair) to the (fair, fare) was (for, fore, four) dollars, we took our (dear, deer) grandmother (for, four, fore) old times' sake. At the bakery booth she won a sack of (flour, flower). A local florist gave her a (flour, flower) to honor her age. After a solid meal and a light (desert, dessert), we (deserted, desserted) the grounds (for, fore, four) the long trip home.

Write one original sentence for each word you didn't use.

Group Four

heal   Some wounds not even a doctor can *heal*.

heel   Achilles died of a wound in his *heel*.

hear   One can *hear* with his ear.

here   *Here* are the groceries you ordered.

heard   She *heard* the plans through the keyhole.

herd   The *herd* of cattle stood trapped in waist-high snow.

hole   Kenneth's sole had a *hole* in it.

whole   He ate the *whole* thing.

hour   Now is the *hour* to get the job done.

our   *Our* dog needs a new collar.

Write a paragraph using the words that are pictured here.

Group Five

knew   She *knew* he was lying.

new   His *new* watchband was too small.

knight   The white *knight* wielded his sword.

night   The burglars entered by dark of *night*.

know   Do you *know* that old song?

no   *No,* I do not.

lead   He died of *lead* poisoning.
Follow the *lead* of your star.

led   The flock of birds was *led* by the strongest.

loose   Use only a *loose* noose.

lose   Did you *lose* the fuse?

One (night, knight) we were (lead, led) through the darkness to a door with a (loose, lose) knob. I was sure we would (lose, loose) our way, but (know, no), our brave leader (knew, new) the way. I didn't (know, no) that (no, know) one was around, so I picked up a (lead, led) pipe for protection. It was a (knew, new) experience.

Write a sentence with the two words that you didn't use.

Group Six

maid   The *maid* wore a pert white apron.

made   Bob *made* a bookcase for $20.

mail   His *mail* was missing a stamp.

male   Are you a *male* chauvinist?

meat   How much *meat* can you eat?

meet   Can you *meet* the public with poise?

one   Are you the *one* who called last night?

won   She *won* $5000 in the lottery.

pail   During the storm, they had to carry water by *pail*.

pale   She painted the walls a *pale* green.

The (maid, made) entered the store where a young (mail, male) butcher stood behind the (meet, meat) counter. "Did we (meat, meet) before?" he asked.

"No," she answered. "I'm the (one, won) who (won, one) the lottery ticket you sent me by (mail, male)."

The boy grew (pale, pail) and (made, maid) a slight noise in his throat. "Glad to (meat, meet) you," he said sheepishly.

Group Seven

pair	Jan brought a *pair* of walking shoes.
pare	You need not *pare* cucumbers at all.
pear	The *pear* was succulent and sweet.
passed	Jack whistled as he *passed* the haunted house. (Think *-ed* form of the *verb*)
past	The children should not be up *past* eight. The church is *past* the river. (Think *beyond*.)
piece	Is this your second *piece* of pie?
peace	Christmas is a season of *peace*.
plain	Tell me in *plain* English what it means. The "buffalo" on the *plain* were really bison.
plane	His *plane* dipped gracefully into the dive. He used a *plane* to level the door.
principal	Air pollution may be the *principal* cause of lung cancer. The *principal* paid off the *principal* on the school debt.
principle	He acted on *principle* even under stress. (Think ru*le*.)

The (principal, principle) witnesses of the (plane, plain) crash said that the ship took off from the (plain, plane). It successfully (passed, past) the first mountain, but then just (pared, paired) the second before a huge explosion disturbed the (piece, peace) of the area. The (principle, principal) cause of the crash is still under investigation.

Write a sentence with each of the words you didn't use here.

Group Eight

quiet	The cast maintained perfect *quiet* backstage.
quite	She was *quite* taken aback by the gift.

rain   *Rain* and sleet were predicted for the holiday week-end.

rein   With a tug on the *rein*, she was riding free.

reign   The monarch's *reign* was brief. (Think king, reign.)

rap   Even a light *rap* on the door will rouse the butler.

wrap   Did she *wrap* Grandpa's socks in Mom's package?

red   Danny has *red* hair.

read   Have you *read* the assignment yet?

right   His *right* hand was paralyzed by a pinched nerve. You have the *right* to remain silent.

rite   The mysterious *rite* included deep bows and anointings.

write   I have three letters to *write* tonight.

ring   The telephone should *ring* at three. He placed the *ring* on his little finger.

wring   Do not *wring* or squeeze the sweater.

A loud (wrap, rap) at the door broke the (quiet, quite) of the house. Then the doorbell sounded a long (wring, ring), but when I went to answer, only a misty evening (rain, reign, rein) confronted me. I began to (wring, ring) my hands, and I was (quite, quiet) sure I was losing my mind when I remembered the (ring, wring) I'd buried in the yard. Throwing on a light (wrap, rap), I darted into the night to perform the weird (rite, write, right). I am happy to be able to (write, right, rite) about it.

Write a sentence with each of the words that you didn't use.

Group Nine

road   The gas station is down the *road* a way.

rode   She *rode* bareback all the way home.

rowed   Bill *rowed* until he thought his arms would fall off.

sale   The sofa was marked half price at the January *sale*.

sail   The *sail* billowed in the brisk breeze.

sea   The *sea* was calm as glass.

see   Can you *see* a distance of twenty feet?

shone   His car *shone* after the wax job.

shown   If you had *shown* me the way, I wouldn't have got lost.

sight   Fields of golden wheat were a happy *sight* to his old eyes.

site   The *site* of their new house was at the top of the hill.

cite   Can you *cite* three passages from scripture?

The sun (shone, shown) so brightly as I (rode, road, rowed) down the (rode, road, rowed) that I couldn't (see, sea). The cool blue water of the (sea, see) was a relief to my strained (sight, site, cite). I took off in my boat and (road, rode, rowed) several miles downstream. Soon, I came to the (sight, site, cite) of an old castle, now up for (sale, sail).

Write a sentence with each of the words you didn't use.

Group Ten

some   *Some* dogs prefer shoes to bones.

sum   Six is the *sum* of two and four.

son   Solomon was the *son* of David.

sun   The *sun* may replace oil for fuel.

stationary They dyed the curtains in the *stationary* tubs. (Think *a*, *attached*.)

stationery She used scented *stationery* for her correspondence. (Think *e*, *envelopes*.)

steal   See if you can *steal* a cookie or two.

steel   The bridge was constructed of *steel*. *Steel* yourself for the next ordeal.

tail   The squirrel's *tail* twitched nervously.

tale   Gramps could spin a *tale* an hour long.

1. (Some, sum) of the (stationery, stationary) is gone.
2. One clerk was caught (steeling, stealing) (some, sum).
3. He left it on the (steel, steal) desk.
4. My (son, sun) saw the dog with his (tail, tale) between his legs.
5. According to the (tale, tail) she told, they are (sun, son) worshippers.

Make a choice for each blank space.

bare, bear	**1.** I can't ____ to ____ the facts.
heel, heal	**2.** Will that salve ____ the wound in his ____ ?
pare, pair, pear	**3.** He doesn't know how to ____ a ____ .
reign, rain, rein	**4.** The ____ of the king began in a heavy ____ .
cite, site	**5.** Is this the ____ of the battle?
ate, eight	**6.** We ____ dinner at ____ o'clock.
bored, board	**7.** We were ____ with the non-news on the bulletin ____ .
meat, meet	**8.** Can I ____ you at the ____ counter?
read, red	**9.** I ____ "Little ____ Riding Hood" in the second grade.
ring, wring	**10.** If you ____ me once more, I'll ____ your neck.
road, rode, rowed	**11.** Some ____ down the river; others ____ the ____ .
quiet, quite	**12.** The church was ____ and cool.
pare, pair, pear	**13.** A ____ of pants costs a small fortune.
reign, rein, rain	**14.** This horse knows who holds the ____ .

TROUBLE WORDS

Twelve homonyms in the English language seem to give people more trouble than all the other words they know. They need special attention and plenty of practice.

Watch out! Don't trip on these two.

you're = you are	*You're* looking well.
your = possessive pronoun	*Your* books are overdue.

Possessive pronouns are one kind of determiner. See page 15.

Decide which form fits each sentence.

1. I like my car better than ____ car.
2. Well, ____ interior is classier.
3. But ____ motor is better.
4. ____ a keen observer.
5. ____ car doesn't skip like mine.
6. ____ probably doing something wrong.
7. ____ paint job is smoother, too.
8. ____ going to pay extra for mileage.

9. How many miles does _____ car get to a gallon?

10. Less than _____ economy model, I'm sure.

These sound-alike words and exercises appeared in an 1873 spelling book. What words are strange to you? Your dictionary should tell you if they are archaic or out of date.

ALE, a malt liquor.
AIL, to trouble; to distress.

AIR, the fluid we breathe.
ERE, before.
EYRE, a court of circuit judges.
HÊIR, one who inherits.

AUGHT, any thing.
OUGHT, in duty bound.

AWN, the beard of corn.
AULN, a French measure; an ell.

BALD, without hair.
BAWL ED, *did* bawl; cried aloud.

BALE, a pack of goods.
BAIL, a surety.

BALL, a round body.
BAWL, to cry or speak aloud.

BARB, the down of plants; beard.
BARBE, armor of leather for horses.

BATE, to abate; to deduct.
BAIT, a lure; to harass.

BAIZE, a coarse woolen stuff.
BAYS, a garland, or chaplet.

BÂRE, nude; naked.
BEÂR, an animal; to suffer.

BASE, vile; mean.
BASS, the gravest part of music.

SENTENCES CONTAINING SOME OF THE FOREGOING WORDS.

1. What does *ail* that man? Has he been drinking *ale*? That is *ail*-ment enough.

2. The *heir* is in poor health, and has gone to try the mountain *air*. He is a student of law, and purposes, *ere* he reaches manhood, to prepare himself to serve as a judge in *eyre*.

3. If a brother offend in *aught*, we *ought*, if he be penitent, freely to forgive him; for thus saith the Lord: "If thy brother trespass against thee, rebuke him; and, if he repent, forgive him." A great poet says: "To err is human, to forgive divine."

4.
> The culprit stole a *bale* of goods,
>   Which landed him in jail:
> He then gave up the *bale* of goods,
>   But could not give good *bail*.

5. *Baize*, though nothing but coarse cloth, is sometimes the covering of higher merit, than that which is honored with *bays*, or chaplets of any kind.

6. The *bear* is sometimes made to leap or dance by placing him with *bare* feet on heated plates of iron, so that he can not *bear* to stand still. This is cruel sport.

Another group of trouble words can be even more confusing because there are three homonyms.

More on how to spell contractions on page 105.

they're = they are	*They're going skiing.*
their = possessive pronoun	*Their mittens were lost.*
there = place	I put the poster *there*.

Choose among *there*, *their* and *they're* for each sentence.

1. I want ＿＿ names as soon as possible.
2. ＿＿ drinks are on the table.
3. I told you to go ＿＿ and never return.
4. ＿＿ it is, all in one package.
5. Is ＿＿ going to be a snowstorm?
6. Do you think ＿＿ going to arrive on time?
7. ＿＿ just isn't time to do everything.
8. I told you no, so ＿＿ !
9. ＿＿ on ＿＿ way here now!
10. When they return, ＿＿ going to clean up this mess.

Perhaps the toughest pair of trouble words is this.

it's = it is	*It's a big night for her.*
its = possessive pronoun	The kitten has lost *its* mitten.

Which form, *its* or *it's*, should be used in each sentence?

1. Look, ＿＿ a snowman!
2. Let's tweak ＿＿ carrot nose.
3. Do you think ＿＿ a good idea?
4. ＿＿ not the type to talk back.
5. On, come on, ＿＿ okay.
6. ＿＿ owner might complain.
7. Aw, ＿＿ only a little kid.
8. Well, ＿＿ Sunday.
9. ＿＿ going to melt anyway.
10. ＿＿ head will melt first.

Here's another pair of homonyms to remember.

who's = who is	*Who's coming with me?*
whose = possessive pronoun	*Whose box is that?*

1. ____ going to break the news to him?
2. It's his job. That's ____ job it is.
3. Are those the girls ____ coats were stolen?
4. ____ going to call the police?
5. ____ responsibility is it to contact the authorities?
6. I don't know ____ going with us tomorrow.
7. ____ there?
8. I don't know ____ supposed to do it.
9. That's the woman ____ house is on fire.
10. ____ in charge here?

Keep in mind that possessive pronouns **never** have apostrophes.

You may have noticed that all the trouble words are alike in one way. One word in each pair is a possessive pronoun (your, its, their, whose) and the other word is a contraction (you're, it's, they're, who's). The last group is not like the others. These are three common sound-alike words, but no contractions or pronouns.

to—I go *to* night class.

two—I am getting *two* credit hours.

too—Why don't you come, *too*? (Think also or extra o.)

1. I want ____ rest.
2. Is it ____ much ____ ask?
3. ____ goblets were smashed.
4. Oh, that's ____ bad.
5. I want ____ know how it happened.
6. Yes, I'd like ____ know, ____ .
7. ____ clumsy people were involved, the mailman and me.
8. You were probably in ____ much of a hurry.
9. I tried ____ catch them, but they fell.
10. That's going ____ cost you ____ weeks' allowance.
11. Don't be ____ generous.
12. I'm only trying ____ help you.
13. Can you give me ____ dollars?
14. ____ each his own.
15. You're ____ careless with money.

The only way to be sure the twelve trouble words are firm in your mind is to practice using them. Decide which word should be used in each case, following this code:

> **th** — their, they're, or there
> **t** — to, too, two
> **y** — you're or your
> **w** — who's or whose
> **i** — it's or its

1. **I** going to be a dull party.
2. **W** mother died?
3. **Th** aren't a lot of people here.
4. Cut off **y** pigtails and curl **y** hair.
5. I want **th** shoes wiped clean.
6. January is **t** cold.
7. I like **y** car better than mine.
8. **I** a shame **y** **t** late for the pie.
9. Tell me **y** name.
10. Lie **th** a minute.
11. **I** six o'clock.
12. I know **y** eyes are closed.
13. Do you think **i** all right to cross now?
14. **I** **t** bad you missed the first act.
15. I left **i** sweater at the kennel.
16. **Th** going to paint the kitchen next.
17. Let me guide you **th**.
18. I want mine **t** be chocolate.
19. **W** hiking shoes are these?
20. **Y** so brisk and cheerful.
21. **W** asking the questions here?
22. **Y** a good boy, Brian!
23. Don't be **t** sure!
24. **Th** is still a lot you can do for him.
25. Postage is going up **t** cents.

If you had all twenty-five right, you shouldn't have any trouble with the next group. Decide for yourself which of the twelve trouble words fits.

1. I like mine better than _____ .

2. This problem is _____ easy _____ be a challenge.
3. I want to go _____ the party.
4. _____ a big pest!
5. I want to know _____ sock sizes.
6. Are these _____ shoes or _____ shoes?
7. You don't look _____ happy about it.
8. Whoopee! Now I know _____ mad!
9. It snowed _____ much this winter.
10. _____ is no use crying over spilled milk.
11. _____ sweater is this?
12. I choose my clothes, you choose _____ own.
13. _____ kidding.
14. _____ a bad test.
15. Tell me what _____ wearing tonight.
16. I went _____ to meet _____ mothers.
17. _____ got my pen?
18. He's _____ young _____ see this film.
19. I heard _____ going fishing.
20. The dog bit _____ own tail.
21. Give me _____ hand.
22. _____ afraid of the big bad wolf?
23. _____ crazy for sure!
24. Those are _____ words, not mine.
25. _____ all right with me if you go.

Put on your editor's cap and proofread the following paragraphs for mistakes. Rewrite the paragraphs.

With it's ears hanging low and its tail between it's legs, the mongrel flopped after the children. In obedience to they're mother, they shooed the dog away, but their commands were only half-hearted. They knew it didn't belong two any of there friends. They wondered who's dog he was. The dog's actions showed that he knew they're real desires.

Ever since they'd lost Ricky who had to be put to sleep after the mowers' blade cut off his ear, the children envied everyone else's dogs. For too cents they would have carried this mutt home with them now, but their mother's warning sounded in there ears: "I don't care who's dog he was. Your not bringing any dogs into this house." And so they chased him away while half inviting him too stay.

Write an original paragraph about this scene using at least five possessives correctly.

How to CAPITALIZE all the words in the English language with style and sincerity ~ ~ ~ and do it right.

Capital letters aren't just for looks. Every capital is like a spotlight on a word. In some languages, capital letters highlight all important words. In American English, however, capitals have only two basic uses.

Capitals signal sentence beginnings.

Capitals distinguish particular or "proper" names of persons, places and things from common nouns.

The first position anywhere is often the highest and most important. In writing, the first word is important enough to merit a capital letter. Here are some of the first words that should be capitalized.

Capitalize I (the most important person to myself) and O (but not oh).	Should *I* wait at the gate?
	I've waited for you, *O* bright yellow moon.
	The medal is beautiful, but *oh*, at what price was it earned!

Find the words that should be capitalized.

1. Will i know by Wednesday?
2. The word should come by, oh, perhaps Tuesday.
3. i'll send the report and, oh, the X-rays, too.
4. i wanted so much, o good doctor, to hear you say that.
5. Can i take you home now?

Capitalize the first word of every sentence.

No I asked for a pillow the nurse brought it.

yes I asked for a pillow. The nurse brought it.

Supply the capitals.

Becky loves her dog actually she idolizes him why shouldn't she she saved for a year to pay for him his license and food and obedience lessons come out of her own pocket too she spends hours with him daily practically all the training and love he receives comes from her no wonder he loves her too.

Confused about fragments? Go back to page 53. For sentence punctuation, go ahead to page 89.

Which of the words in these groups should be capitalized? Be sure you identify complete sentences.

1. new Orleans is a city of contradictions it is a split personality.
2. many of its streets as you walk down them resemble alleys.
3. some older areas even give the appearance of slums or business districts.
4. between which are quaint little pastry and gift shops.
5. beyond dismal doors however are hidden gardens of great charm.
6. hotels are elegant with marble corridors lined with southern style majestic columns and windows hung with magnificent Austrian drapes.
7. restaurants everywhere are famous for gourmet French and Italian or Southern, old-fashioned, "homestyle" cooking.
8. still, lining the central street skyscrapers and geometric structures are as modern as in any city in the States.
9. every contemporary store has its quaint variation giving it a unique personality.
10. for example Woolworth's has Spanish metal grillwork ornamentation.

Write ten sentences about a city like this one or another place you know.

Capitalize the first word of every complete sentence of a direct quote.

"Will you wash the dishes, Bert?" his roommate asked. (exact words spoken)

"Why should I wash them? Didn't I cook the meal?" Bert responded. (*Didn't* begins a new sentence.)

"I know," his roommate continued, "but I have an important meeting in five minutes." (*But* is not the first word of a directly quoted sentence.)

Supply the capitals needed.

1. "can't we agree on anything?" screamed Lynn.

2. "the first thing we'd better do," returned Del, "is calm down and talk things out."

3. "so who's excited? you're the one who's always contradicting me," Lynn said.

4. Still calm, Del argued that the main cause of their squabbles was getting excited too fast.

5. After a while Lynn agreed, but added, "it's only that you make me so mad when you constantly oppose everything I say."

6. Jill told Jeff to ask the librarian if they have *Sports Illustrated*.

7. "do you have *Sports Illustrated*? asked Jeff. "it isn't with the magazines."

Capitalize the first word in the salutation of a letter.	*Gentlemen:* *My dear Joan,* *Dear Uncle Bill,* (*Uncle Bill* is capitalized because it is a name.)

Capitalize only the first word of the complimentary close of a letter.	*Cordially yours,* *Your grateful and loving friend,* *Yours very truly,* *Most sincerely yours,*

Supply the needed capitals.

1. sincerely yours,

2. my dear friend Jezebel,

3. dear Aunt Mildred,

4. your respectful son,

5. my dearest grandmother,

6. your loving dad,

7. your concerned and devoted friend,

8. Allison dear,

9. very truly yours,

10. gratefully and lovingly yours,

Set up a letter. Use blank lines for everything except the salutation and the complimentary close.

Rewrite the following letter, supplying the needed capitals.

my dear Joanne,

o cruel fate! wouldn't you know it i've got the measles! yes, measles, the childhood disease i'm sitting thinking how lucky i am to be going on a ski trip to Canada this week suddenly my eyes are very tired and i notice a rash on my forearm.

"mom," i yell, "what did we have for dinner?" then . . . oh, what's the use? to make a long story short, as i said, i am covered with red blotches.

needless to say, the ski trip is off reading is off TV is off and soon i'm going to be off, if you know what i mean. don't let my tragedy ruin your fun, though, and bring me a souvenir.

your friend in red mourning,

Terri

Write a brief letter to a long-lost friend whom you learned has won a national prize in science.

You can review common and proper nouns on page 18.

Being Particular

The second main use of capitals is to distinguish particular persons, places and things, or proper nouns, from common nouns. To discover your ability to recognize the difference between particular and common things, see if you can identify the *particular* noun in each pair of nouns below. On your paper write the *particular* word, capitalizing it.

For example: organization (common) Parent Teacher Board (proper)

school	newspaper	freshman
public school #1	the times	dan jacobs
northwest territory	girl	book
territory	marsha jones	*the turn of the screw*
river	twin towers	geography
jordan river	skyscraper	geography I
document	monkey	month
declaration of independence	blippo	february
general	country	planet
old hickory	england	mars
the governor	(go) west (on 3rd st.)	chinese
governor alfred e smith	the west	race
weekend	bible	coach machock
saturday	prayerbook	jim machock

If you scored 20 correct, you won't have trouble with capitals.

Capitalize proper nouns. A proper noun is the name of a particular person, place, thing or idea.

Bill Jones   boy

Melanie Mercado   girl

Delaware   state

Spotty   beagle

Write sentences about these pictures identifying the proper nouns by capital letters.

Capitalize the names of persons. Besides being careful to spell names correctly (Ann, Anne, Smith, Smythe, Smyth), learn whether a name contains more than one capital.

Raymondo de la Pena   Pat McDonald   Gretchen O'Rourke

Capitalize the names of particular places.

Streets: Pine Street, Sixty-fourth Street (In hyphenated streets, the second word is not capital.)

avenues: Washington Avenue

boulevards: Mencken Boulevard

drives: Winston Drive

courts: Park Court, Thurman Place

roads: Pennsylvania Turnpike

precincts: Fourth Precinct

wards: Ward 7

squares: Hamilton Square

canyons: Grand Canyon

capes: Cape of Good Hope

dams: Grand Coulee Dam

hills: Bunker Hill

islands: Philippine Islands

cities: Cleveland, Vatican City

counties: Lorain County

districts: Vieux Carré

states: South Dakota

countries: Dominion of Canada

continents: South America

hemispheres: Western Hemisphere

seas: Mediterranean Sea

oceans: Pacific Ocean

parks: Metropolitan State Park

ranges: Rocky Mountains

mountains: Pike's Peak

lakes: Lake Michigan

gulfs: Gulf of New Mexico

valleys: Death Valley

political divisions: Northwest Territory

buildings: Terminal Tower

geographical areas: the Middle East

Do not capitalize east, west, south and north when they refer to directions, only when they refer to a section of the country.

Turn *west* at the first light.

Azaleas grow well on the *east* side of the house.

We were going *north* when the car struck us.

We are going skiing up *North*.

Imagine that the following are envelope addresses. Supply the capitals.

1. 2743 scranton road
   beldon, california

2. 11545 heath road, north
   chesterland, ohio

3. 85 east seventh street
   berlin, massachusetts

4. 116 belvedere boulevard
   saxon, virginia

5. 36 hampton square, apt. #6
   sidney, new jersey

6. 4511 wetzel place
   johnston, pennsylvania

7. 4503 lakeland court
   annandale, tennessee

8. 23685 dixie highway
   fairfax, kentucky

9. p. o. box 400
   new york, new york

10. 850 caxton building
    rochester, new york

Copy the correct form in each pair onto your paper. In some pairs both items are wrong; write those items correctly.

1. a. Northwest Territory
   b. Northwest territory

2. a. Go south till you see a church.
   b. Go South, till you see a church.

3. a. Fifty-first street
   b. Fifty-First Street

4. a. The brooklyn bridge
   b. the Brooklyn Bridge

5. a. the Great Western divide
   b. the Great Western Divide

6. a. Strait of Gibraltar
   b. strait of Gibraltar

7. a. Mount Everest
   b. mount Everest

8. a. Ohio State penitentiary
   b. Ohio State Penitentiary

9. a. Rocky Mountain National Park
   b. Rocky Mountain national park

10. a. Virginia beach
    b. Virginia Beach

Capitalize the specific names of eras, historical events and special events.	**Eras:** Middle Ages, Reign of Terror, Victorian Age, Revolutionary Period
	Historical events: the Reformation, the Boxer Rebellion
	Special events: Winter Olympics, Christmas Dance, Woman's National Outdoor Track and Field Meet

Correctly capitalize the following words on your own paper.

1. women's amateur golf match
2. world war II
3. the world series
4. counter-reformation
5. new stone age
6. chicago fire
7. modern age
8. battle of wounded knee
9. nascar grand national races
10. the winter olympics
11. spanish-american war
12. battle of lexington
13. war of the roses
14. french revolution
15. industrial age
16. contemporary period
17. world food conference
18. romantic age
19. dark ages
20. kentucky derby

Capitalize the names of calendar events.	**days of the week:** Tuesday, Sunday
	months of the year: January, December
	holidays: Fourth of July, Rosh Hashana

Do not capitalize common words related to time.

day   year   era   month   week   century   age

Do not capitalize the four seasons.

summer   winter   spring   fall   autumn

Which words in the following paragraph should be capitalized?

Almost every month in the year contains a holiday or special event or season. The year opens with new year's day. In february lincoln's and washington's birthdays occur together with ground hog day and valentine's day. The month of march brings lent which begins on ash wednesday in february and usually ends in april with easter. The same time of year means passover, too. In mid-march come st. patrick's day and the first day of spring. At the end of may, we celebrate memorial day, and everyone looks ahead to summer.

Write an original paragraph in which you make a survey of the birthdays and important anniversaries of all the members of your family.

Capitalize the names of special identifications.

languages: French, English

peoples: Goths, Anglo-Saxons, Asians

races: Caucasian, Negro, Mongolian

nationalities: Malaysian, Dutch

religions: Baptist, Hindu

Do not capitalize the common words: language, people, tribe.

Write on your paper the words that should be capitalized.

Consider the confusion that would occur at a world conference of peoples. Since there would be representatives from every nation in the world, many languages would be heard on the floor: the european languages — english, french, german, greek, italian, portuguese, dutch, danish, flemish, norwegian, finnish, swiss, spanish, polish, slovak, slovenian, czech and hungarian. Then from the middle east would come the arabic, hebrew, lebanese, turkish, and persian. From south asia you would hear hindi, urdu, malay and bengali, and from southeast asia, vietnamese, burmese, sudanese, pidgin english, indonesian, javanese and balinese. From the far east you would encounter chinese, nepali, japanese, korean, mongolian, tibetan.

To add to the problem, the three main races, negroid, mongoloid and caucasoid with all their variations would be represented as well as many religions including christian: roman catholic, eastern orthodox and protestant. There would be the other major world religions, too: jewish, moslem, zoroastrian, shinto, taoist, confucian, buddhist and hindu. Would any interpreter ever be able to untangle the common problems of so many peoples?

Capitalize the important words in business and political events and organizations.

organizations: Veterans of Foreign Wars

business corporations: Republic Steel, United Airlines

institutions: Spencer Business College, Northwood Junior High School, Ohio State University, Social Studies Department

government bodies: Farm Labor Board, U. S. Army, Supreme Court, Department of the Interior, Congress, Senate

political parties: Democratic party, Labor party

documents: U. S. Constitution, Treaty of Versailles

awards: Pulitzer Prize

Do not capitalize such words as *school, college, motel* or *high school* unless they are part of the proper name.

South High School   the high school student

Stay-Put Motel   a motel on I-71

Supply the needed capitals.

1.   The republicans held a majority in both senate and congress. Two-thirds of the supreme court had been appointed by the republican president and members of the cabinet were chiefly republican. The democratic party will have a hard time passing any bills they want to get through.

2.   Bernadette was a popular and active girl at Wells, holding offices in the student council and school publication. She was chair-person of the spanish club entertainment committee and still found time to work part-time at hess pharmacy. During long holidays she clerked at the local post office in her hometown where as a teenager she had attended thoreau high school.

Write a biographical sketch of yourself or of someone you know revealing all organizations, prizes, jobs and political affiliations.

Capitalize the names of specific vehicles.

ships: HMS Pinafore

planes: Boeing 747

cars: Dodge Omni

spaceships: Gemini XIII

satellites: Syncom

Finish this paragraph by creating fantasy trips for them: The rock group had a lot of travel experience. . . .

Write the words that should be capitalized in your notebook.

Manned space flights were dominated by the russians in the early sixties. Yuri Gagarin manned vostok I. The Russian ship vostok II orbited earth sixteen times before John Glenn went around the world three times in mercury atlas 6. Then vostok III and IV circled the globe 105 times; it took three U.S. attempts on mercury atlas 8 and 9 to make forty revolutions. But after 1965, U.S. gemini ships surpassed U.S.S.R. efforts in soyuz 1 which crashed in 1967. Since then further models of soyuz and apollo spacecraft have been launched. Finally russian and american scientists pooled their efforts on joint projects.

Capitalize trade names but not the common names of products that follow them.

Campbell soup   Dupont nylon   Sohio station

Write a few sentences using the products pictured.

Copy each paragraph, inserting capital letters.

1. Indonesia consists of five large and more than 3000 small islands which form an arc between asia and australia. Its population is chiefly malayan and papuan, but many chinese have settled there also. Its chief language is bahasa indonesian which is a form of malay. The second language which is taught in the schools is english.

2. Chiefly of moslem religion, indonesians are only about ten percent christian. The people on the island of bali have kept their buddhist hindu faith. The country shares borders with malaysian, portuguese and australian territories.

3. The united states has had sixteen presidents who were members of the republican party and thirteen who were democrats. The first two presidents were federalist and the next four were members of the democratic-republican party. Four in the later 1700's belonged to the whig party.

Write all the items that need capitalizing. Write _C_ after words or phrases that are correct.

1. adirondack mountains
2. dumont-durville h.s.
3. darius the great
4. puget sound
5. washington, d.c.
6. ohio-allegheny river
7. the great lakes
8. the language department
9. the gulf of mexico
10. harvard university
11. west of the rockies
12. the laurentian plain
13. the central plateau
14. the arctic slope
15. the house of representatives
16. st. theresa academy
17. the public high school
18. the gunpowder plot
19. a great dane
20. pro-labor
21. in room 114
22. in the spring
23. kennedy freeway
24. salt lake city, utah
25. general motors
26. civil war period
27. lorain county
28. un-american

Search out the words that should be capitalized.

1. When the early fathers signed the declaration of independence in a congress held after the american revolution in philadelphia, did they know that the seat of the government would later be moved to washington, d.c.?

2. Betty, who is a junior at jane addams high school in abbeville, georgia, takes a program including typing III, advanced stenography and business law. She also takes a course in accounting.

3. For breakfast Al always has a glass of tang, a bowl of Kellogg's rice crispies, a slice of wonder bread and swift's sausage.

4. The first national bank building replaced the masonic auditorium on the old ely estate at the intersection of superior and thirty-fifth street.

5. After six days at sea on the ambassador, from wednesday, july 7, to tuesday july 12, they flew by boeing jet to chicago, illinois. From there they were driven in a pontiac to the heart of the city.

6. A team of russian and american astronauts are cooperating on a plan to launch the satellite taurus I from the moon toward mars next fall.

7. You can pick up the ohio turnpike from route 57 just after you cross cascade bridge overlooking the black river and just before oberlin road intersects it.

8. If the groundhog sees his shadow on february 2, groundhog's day, it is said winter will last six weeks longer.

9. The construction of the new innerbelt will cut through the irish, italian and german neighborhoods.

10. Both democrats and republicans rallied to the side of the senator who did all he could to subsidize the schools in the appalachian area of tennessee.

Match each face
with one of these
sentences.

1. That's right.

2. That's *right!*

3. *That's right?*

Put Your Mark on It

Notice how emotions—anger, happiness, fear, uncertainty—can be revealed through punctuation. A period at the end of a sentence is factual and serious. But an exclamation point gives you a completely different reading.

When you speak, your voice gives meaning to your words. You pause or raise your voice, you emphasize certain words or try out a foreign accent. Punctuation marks have to do the same job for your writing. Punctuation makes meaning clear.

Read each of these sentences quickly. What do they mean?

Flowers send him to the hospital quickly.

The administration said the college press is biased.

The secretaries who are on vacation will receive a raise.

Without punctuation you may have a hard time figuring out which of several meanings the sentences are supposed to have. Did you read them this way?

Flowers, send him to the hospital quickly!

The administration, said the college press, is biased.

The secretaries, who are vacation, will receive a raise.

HOW WILL YOU END UP (AFTER ALL)?

Only three marks of punctuation are used to signal the end of a sentence or complete thought: periods, question marks and exclamation points. End marks signal a full stop in reading. They close a sentence or thought and give you some direction about reading it. Most sentences end with a period, showing a drop in voice.

You don't use a period after a direct question or a very strong exclamation.

Use a period after a sentence that makes a statement or gives a command.	**Direct statement:** The Lone Ranger rides again.
	Direct question: Will the Lone Ranger ride again?
	Strong exclamation: Hurry, Tonto!

These are some kinds of sentences that should be finished with a period.

Indirect statement: He reported that the Dow-Jones average rose sixteen points today.

Indirect question: The dentist asked Mr. Tramantano if he was   allergic to Novocain.

Polite request: Will you please hand me the sports section, Albert.

Command: Stay out of drafts.

Write one sentence of your own for each kind of sentence shown.

Use a question mark to end a sentence that asks a direct question.	How did you do it? *not* He asked how you did it.
	Is dinner ready yet? *not* I want to know if dinner is ready.

Questions usually begin with interrogatives—*who, what, where, when* and *how*—or with auxiliaries—forms of *be* or *have*.

Identify any direct questions below by rewriting the sentence and adding the question mark. Rewrite any statements as questions and add question marks.

1. How does he like his steak
2. He likes it rare
3. Jack is a good cook
4. Will you hold the candle while I light it
5. When is the steak coming

Use an exclamation point to end a sentence, word or phrase that expresses strong emotion.	**Sentence:**　Come at once!　My brother is drowning! **Phrase:**　Not Billy!　Quick, in the barn! **Word:**　Gosh!　Hurry!

Supply one of the three end marks wherever they are needed. Watch out for sentence fragments!

1. The skiff teetered dangerously in the wind
2. Come here, Bill
3. Can you lend a hand
4. I asked if you could help me
5. I don't know the first thing about managing a sailboat
6. Much less in stormy waters
7. Then just sit down and stay out of the way
8. Wow Lou I almost lost my balance
9. Look a funnel is forming in the West
10. Bill, are you ready to call it quits
11. How I wish I'd taken Mr. Green's advice
12. What was that
13. To drive across the country
14. Well, it's too late now Grab that rope, will you
15. Now, pull as hard as you can
16. Is that the best you can do
17. I'm pulling as hard as I can
18. What else do you want
19. Just hold it
20. Quick ease up on the rope
21. I wonder if we'll ever make it back to shore
22. Lou Lou the funnel is passing the other way
23. Now maybe we have a chance

24. Not unless you control that sail, Bill

25. I think we'll make it after all, Mary Lou

26. Remind me not to go sailing with you again

27. Are you sorry I came

Review sentence fragments on page 53.

Supply the needed end marks for the following paragraph. Write just the words that should precede and follow each mark.

Help thief somebody stole my shoe Usher, can you direct your light into this row under the seat I asked if you would flash that light here I want to check whether I lost my shoe I know I came in with two of them Ouch You are standing on my foot you oaf Here look on this side I see something shiny

The Latest Thing

A reading book from 1871 taught these punctuation marks. Which ones are no longer used? Which are used only in printed books?

The *Caret* ∧ shows where words are to be put in, that have been omitted by mistake; as, Live ∧ᶦⁿ peace.

The *Diæresis* is placed over the latter of two vowels, to show that they belong to two distinct syllables; as, aërial.

The *Hyphen* - is used to connect compound words; as, Well-doing; or the parts of a word separated at the end of a line.

The *Index* ☞ points to something special or remarkable; as, ☞ Important News!

The *Ellipsis* **** . . . . or —— shows that certain words or letters have been purposely omitted; as, K...g, k . . . g, or k——g, for king.

The *Paragraph* ¶ denotes the beginning of a new subject. It is used chiefly in the Bible; as, ¶ The same day came to him, etc.

The *Section* § is used to divide a book or chapter into parts; as, § 45.

The *Asterisk,* * the *Obelisk,* † the *Double Dagger,* ‡ and sometimes other marks,* refer to notes in the margin.

---

* For instance: the Section mark, §, and the Parallel, ‖

HOW TO USE COMMAS

You can't go through life using only periods, question marks and exclamation points in your writing. Language control includes using punctuation within a sentence to control your meaning. Commas are the marks of punctuation that most people have trouble with. Using too many commas can cause just as much confusion as not using enough. All you have to do is learn a few simple rules and follow them.

Separate the items in addresses and dates with commas. In a sentence, use a comma after the last item.	Atlanta, Georgia, is different from New Orleans. 3388 Park Avenue, Willoughby, North Dakota, is my address. Grace never expected Friday, June 13, to be her wedding day. April 23 is Shakespeare's birthday. (No comma when there is only one item.)

Write down the words that should be followed by commas in these sentences.

1. Was your visit to Saginaw Michigan profitable?
2. Greenfield Illinois preserves ancient crafts.
3. His residence on 3345 Lake Avenue Berkley burned to the ground.
4. Jerry has been to London several times.
5. The Thames in London England is a city boundary.

Write an original sentence placing the name of the city and state you were born in at the beginning of a sentence.

Where do commas belong in these sentences?

1. April 12 1906 is my mother's birth date.
2. The fanatic predicted that May 13 1998 would be the end of the world.
3. Will you be home on January 27 or 28?
4. On Saturday November 15 I will visit you.
5. February 2 is Groundhog Day.

Write a sentence beginning with the date (month and year) of your birth.

Follow the salutation and the complimentary close of a friendly letter with a comma.	Dear Jan, Hello Old Pal, Sincerely yours, Yours truly,

Copy the words after which commas are required for separating any short items. If no comma is needed, write *No Comma* on your sheet.

1. My old friend and comrade in mischief
2. Tuesday October 31 Marcia will hold a Halloween party.
3. Have you ever been to New England or the South?
4. Washington D.C. is the hub of the government.
5. Chicago Illinois has been called the crossroads of American railways.
6. Oberlin Ohio has a world-famous music conservatory.
7. Is 345 Gulf Road New Haven your correct address?
8. Gratefully yours
9. Hello Dolly
10. Elyria is the golf ball center of the world.
11. I thought you said 798 Vega Avenue was the new address.
12. Eleanor bought a 1981 Honda.
13. On October 15 1875 there was a solar eclipse.
14. On March 15 we commemorate the death of Julius Caesar.
15. On July 14 1789 the French stormed the Bastille.
16. A package arrived from Paris France.
17. Were you planning to include Cambridge Ohio in your trip?
18. Scottsbluff Nebraska is near North Platt.
19. Mark Twain mentions Cairo Illinois in *Huckleberry Finn.*
20. Winesburg Ohio is the subject of Sherwood Anderson's poem.

Write a brief letter to someone at least 100 miles away, extending an invitation to take a summer camping trip with you.

Use commas to separate items of the same kind used in a series.

Nouns: Bert puts celery, tomatoes, carrots and onions into his beef soup.

Notice that *and* can take the place of the comma between the last two items in a series. The comma may also be left in with the last *and*. . . . celery, tomatoes, carrots, and onions.

Verbs: Fred's car snorted, coughed, sputtered and groaned before it woke up to a healthy hum.

Check page 33 if you're still not sure what an adjective is.

Adjectives: The cake was delicate, moist, tender and tasty.

Adverbs: Cautiously, quietly, slyly and spryly the cat stalked her prey.

Why is there no comma separating the words in this sentence?

Cautiously and slyly the cat stalked her prey.

Find the words in a series and separate them with commas.

1. To make good pizza you need dough tomato sauce cheese oregano and pepperoni.
2. Stuffed cabbage can be baked in water tomato sauce or wine.
3. You can serve apples stewed baked broiled or fried.
4. Carefully accurately and skillfully Molly mixed the ingredients for her special pie filling.
5. The pot hissed rattled spilled over and burned.
6. Greg shivered in the corner, humiliated lonely hungry and afraid.
7. Quietly cautiously slowly and surely Jose made his way through the tunnel.
8. The team uniforms were a bright and cheerful gold.
9. The audience whistled stamped screamed and hissed.

Write one original sentence using words in a series.

Use a comma to separate two or more adjectives that come before a noun.

John was a tall, dark boy.

John was a tall, dark and handsome lad. *or* John was a tall, dark, and handsome lad.

Separate by commas any adjectives in a series that come before the nouns in the sentences below.

1. He brandished a shiny sharp knife for scaling the fish.
2. Putting on a big white apron, he set to work.

3. Working from head to tail with the back of the knife, he scraped the scales.

4. Big heavy drops of sweat poured from his forehead as the scales flew.

5. Having cut away the entrails and head and tail, he made a deep lateral cut to remove the dorsal fin.

Write the words which should be followed by commas in these sentences. If the sentence does not need a comma, write No Comma.

1. The day was pleasant and cool.
2. She loved to pile her sandwiches with pickles relish onion and tomatoes.
3. Hamburger with cheese was his very favorite meal.
4. Slowly deliberately and precisely the watchmaker replaced the parts.
5. Steel yourself for a tough competitive game.
6. Delores could hit pitch and field a ball.
7. Blocking and kicking were his specialties.
8. His specialties included blocking kicking tackling and passing.
9. Margot excelled in tennis and basketball.
10. In his early youthful career he was a model of honesty.

Use a comma to set off introductory elements in a sentence. Use a comma after words like yes, no, well, oh.	Yes, I'll call you at four.
	Why, I didn't know you won't be home.
	Of course, if you prefer I can call at six.
	No, tomorrow will be fine.

Place commas where they are needed in these sentences.

1. Goodness the sun is hot.
2. Yes it feels like 115 in the shade.
3. Well I'm glad we brought something to drink.
4. Darn where's the can opener?
5. Oh no do you mean we can't open the soda?

Write original sentences that begin with *golly, why, gee* and *no.*

Using the verbs runs, jumps, twists, flips, straightens and slices, describe the action in the pictures.

Use a comma to set off names used in direct address. | Phyllis, will you close that window.

There are three positions that nouns in direct address can take in a sentence:

    ___D A___ , will you close that window.

    Will you, ___D A___ , close that window.

    Will you close that window, ___D A___ .

Using the name *Janet*, rewrite the three sentences above.

Write the words after which commas should be placed.

1. Donna you stand over by the bookcase.
2. You Don walk across the stage toward her.
3. Meanwhile you can be peeking in at the window Dan.
4. What expression Dan do you think you will wear?
5. But Don you have to give Dan reason to look jealous.
6. Are you going to exaggerate your jealousy?

Be the director. Direct the people in this scene to act their roles in five sentences that use their names in direct address.

Use the following words in sentences that include direct address. Place each in one of the three positions indicated.

End	Beginning	Middle
mister	Dad	my children
kid	Honey	Sweetie
you little monkey	Mike	Folks
silly	You	dear friends
Eleanor	Loretta	slowpoke

Supply all needed punctuation.

Well Jerry how are things going with the wife children and menagerie The last time I saw you, you looked strapping tall and handsome Goodness now you seem shrunken and withered Jer your hunched drooping posture makes me tired just looking at you What on earth has happened in these twenty years Is there anything I can say do or contribute to help you out old pal

cast
your
spell

605 Westbrook Avnue
Brandon, Florida 33511
August 31, 19__

D. Hamblin & Compeny
48 Delano Avnue
Tampa, Florida 33619

Gentleman:

I read your advertizement in the paper last
nite and am appling for the position of secretery.
I have just gradated from high school with a major
in business. May I request an apointment for an
interview at you're earlist convienance.

Yours truley,

Richard Courier

Richard Courier

If you were the employer who had advertised for a secretary,
would you contact this person? Why or why not?
You will notice that though this letter puts the message across
clearly, poor spelling communicates another message — carelessness.

Measure your spelling ability by taking the test below.

1. (silent) quiet, quite
2. misspell, mispell
3. occured, occurred, ocurred
4. fourty, forty
5. already, allready
6. all right, alright
7. (main) principal, principle
8. mathematics, mathmatics
9. (mislay) loose, lose
10. (present tense) choose, chose
11. friend, freind
12. your, you're (book)
13. its, it's (a girl!)
14. suprise, surprise, surprize
15. equiptment, equipment
16. disappoint, dissappoint
17. (jeans) cloths, clothes, close
18. medecine, medicine
19. (4th) fourth, forth
20. (to go) forward, foreword
21. separate, seperate
22. their, there (song)
23. Wednesday, Wensday
24. (foot) peddle, pedal
25. (car) breaks, brakes
26. buisness, business

Every word that you spelled correctly represents hundreds of others that you already know how to spell. The errors say that you, like everyone else, have trouble with some words. Even though you can spell most of the words you use, no one can memorize all 600,000 words in the English language. It's the troublesome five percent that everybody has to work at.

Don't let a few small letters throw you for a loop. Take the offensive. Attack your spelling problems before they get you down. Here are some ways to help you conquer that troublesome five percent. Some methods will work better for you than others.

EIGHT GREAT WAYS TO IMPROVE YOUR SPELLING

1. Look Hard at the Word — at the individual letters as well as at the whole shape. Is it long or short? Where are the tall letters and the drop letters? Close your eyes and see the word. This method will suit you if you have a good visual memory.

2. Write the Word a) in the air with your whole arm, b) on your palm with your index finger, c) on your paper — large, and then small. Write it until the crossed *t*'s, dotted *i*'s, long *y*'s and tall *l*'s come naturally. Feel the word in your muscles.

3. Say the Word slowly and distinctly, separating the syllables and exaggerating the correct pronunciation. Pronounce even the letters that may be silent if it helps. Spell the word aloud stressing the trouble spots. For instance, for *mortgage*, say *mort-gage*. Force yourself to hear the silent *t*.

Here are some words that may be troublesome if you don't pronounce them correctly. Say each word aloud, breaking it into syllables. Exaggerate the sounds, especially at the problem areas which are in boldface type.

sur prise	re **a** lize	li **bra** ry	at ten d**an**ce
mis chi**e vou**s	bus **i** ness	li **a** ble	hin **dr**ance
gr**ie vou**s	re **al** ly	gram **mar**	en **tr**ance
Ha**l** low een	a**th le** tic	con **ve ni** ent	re mem **br**ance
hun **dre**d	hur ri **ed** ly	dis as **trou**s	**we** ird

1. Which three words end in *ous*?
2. Write the verb form of each of the following: *remembrance, hindrance, entrance.* What is the secret of spelling the changed forms correctly?
3. Which words contain the following words: *real(2), able, mar, dance, we* and *hall*?
4. Which word in the list is capitalized? Why?
5. What are the root words of *mischievous, grievous, Halloween, really, athletic, hurriedly, convenient*?

4. Study the Silent Letters of words. In 1640 all the letters in these words were pronounced. Say the words pronouncing all the sounds.

knicht   often   drought   night   folk   halfe

But English is alive and well and living in the United States. It grows and changes all the time. Sometimes words that have come from other times or places contain letters that are no longer pronounced. There's only one way to go with these words, and that is to memorize them.

Write the following words, supplying the silent partners.

WR

_____ rath, _____ ring, _____ riggle, _____ ry, _____ rote, _____ riting, _____ restle, _____ ritten, _____ rong, _____ retch, _____ ren, _____ reck, _____ reathe, _____ rap, _____ rack, _____ rangle, _____ rist, _____ renched

Fill in the needed word beginning with *wr*

Ronny's face displayed a __1__ (twisted) smile as he __2__ (put down by pen) to his friend about the __3__ (fighting) match in which he __4__ (fastened) up a victory against a long-standing opponent. The poor __5__ (miserable person) __6__ (squirmed) and tried desperately to show his __7__ (anger), but Ron caught him by the __8__ (hand joint) and almost __9__ (twisted) his arm out of its socket. He knew it was __10__ (not right), but he was glad he had __11__ (put down on paper) all the gory details.

KN

knack, knead, knee, knew, knife, knight, knit, knob, knock, knot, know, known.

WH

whack, whale, wham, what, wheat, whee, when, where, whether, which, whiff, while, whine, whip, whirl, whisk, whisker, whisper, whistle, white, whiz, whole, whoop, whose

5. Connect a word with a gimmick to help you remember its spelling.

1. The MEDIC practices MEDICine.
2. It is "BR," cold in FeBRuary.
3. A dependABLE person is ABLE.
4. PotaTOES have eyes, but also TOES.
5. Three E's lie in cEmEtEry.
6. You use Envelopes when you use stationEry.
7. The stationAry tubs are Attached.
8. No booKKeeping without booK and Keeping. (Three double letters in a row.)
9. PERMA is pressed into PERMAnently.
10. No haggy WITCH in sandWICH.
11. A CAFEteria is a little CAFE.
12. The SECRETAry is trained to keep A SECRET.

Have someone dictate the following paragraph to you.

The secretary, who is dependable, and the bookkeeper, who is not, were walking past the cemetery last February. Rather than eat soggy potatoes in the cafeteria, they had each brought a sandwich to work and were now out for a walk. "My hands are so cold," said the secretary, "they are permanently frozen. I'll never be able to address those envelopes."

"Don't worry," said his friend, "I have some medicine at the office that should help."

You can often identify nouns by their ability to be plural. See page 16.

6. Learn to Form Plurals of nouns.
Test your skill by pluralizing the following.

coat	baby	mother-in-law	chief
shoe	bush	monkey	goose
Jones	windmill	Stetson	Japanese
cat	three-year-old	wife	deer

It is not necessary to memorize plurals. A few simple rules will guide you to the correct spelling of hundreds of words.

Most nouns form their plural by adding -s.

book, books	island, islands
chimney, chimneys	curtain, curtains
hand, hands	bottle, bottles

Nouns ending in -s, -sh, -ch and -x and -z form their plural by adding -es.

success, successes	church, churches
bush, bushes	box, boxes

Write the plural form of the following words.

tax	hoax	Smith	brush
birch	address	address	hurrah
thrush	refugee	picture	atlas
cannister	choir	Davis	wish
mother	immigrant	occupant	ditch
house	wax	caress	mass
bench	scratch	crash	dish
bicycle	brick	hairbrush	ticket
dash	pouch	lock	watch
schedule	witch	stitch	patient

process	sash	sandwich	Mr. French
Mr. Ford	fox	prefix	match
circus	genius	actress	eyelash
dress	plane	cent	six
branch	key	latch	grass

Some words end in *-f* or *-fe* or *ff*. Most of them form their plurals by adding *-s*.

roofs	beliefs	tariffs	chefs	handkerchiefs
griefs	sheriffs	dwarfs	safes	cliffs
chiefs	giraffes	rebuffs	proofs	whiffs

A few form their plurals by changing the *f* to *v* and adding *-es*

knife, knives	themselves	half, halves
life, lives	elf, elves	shelf, shelves
wife, wives	thief, thieves	wolf, wolves
self, selves	leaf, leaves	loaf, loaves

Some take either form of plural.

wharf, wharfs, wharves	calf, calfs, calves
scarf, scarfs, scarves	beef, beefs, beeves
hoof, hoofs, hooves	sheaf, sheafs, sheaves

Only eight words change their root to form the plural.

man	men	tooth, teeth
woman	women	louse lice
goose	geese	foot feet
mouse	mice	child children

Only a few words remain the same in the singular and plural forms. They name certain animals and nationalities.

sheep	Japanese	fish	Vietnamese
salmon	Swiss	species	Portuguese
moose	Chinese	trout	Burmese

Pluralize the following.

tariff	child	half	leaf
show-off	loaf	self	by-line
football	old timer	housewife	passer by
foot	dwarf	grief	thief
trout	life	giraffe	knife
sheriff	wife	calf	godchild
Japanese	elf	handful	cupful
woman	hoof	wisdom tooth	onlooker
jackknife	tap dancer	man	fish
mouse	moose	goose	sheep

Using the numbered words, fill in the slots with the correct plural forms.

1. thief, 2. chef, 3. loaf, 4. calf, 5. teapot, 6. safe, 7. handkerchief, 8. scarf, 9. footprint, 10. leaf, 11. foot, 12. teenager

The __1__ tied up the __2__ outside and stole three __3__ of bread, two __4__, and three antique __5__ from the kitchen. They also took 250 thousand dollars from several __6__ of the hotel. Wiping off their prints with their __7__ and __8__, they disguised their __9__ by running in the __10__. But when only three __11__ from their getaway cars, they were stopped by three __12__ who faced them with hunting rifles.

1. fireman, 2. child, 3. bystander, 4. man, 5. woman, 6. nightshift, 7. firefighter, 8. two-by-four, 9. roof.

The __1__ were carrying the twenty __2__ down one by one. The __3__ who were chiefly __4__ and __5__ who worked the __6__ at two neighboring plants, systematically handed the __7__ __8__ to prop the ladders against the blazing __9__.

1. tradesman, 2. wharf, 3. beef, 4. onlooker, 5. German, 6. Japanese, 7. Chinese, 8. Swiss, 9. Portuguese, 10. species.

As dawn crept up, __1__ gathered at the __2__ to watch the unloading of the huge __3__. Among the __4__ were __5__, __6__, __7__, __8__ and __9__. They all had vested interests in the various __10__ of cattle.

Make the following words plural.

1. tax	**8.** waltz	**1.** church	**8.** prefix
2. brush	**9.** strife	**2.** flood	**9.** chief
3. scratch	**10.** fireman	**3.** paper	**10.** man
4. patient	**11.** house	**4.** puff	**11.** eyelash
5. atlas	**12.** cupful	**5.** crutch	**12.** desk
6. washcloth	**13.** time	**6.** address	**13.** gulf
7. lamp	**14.** widow	**7.** deer	**14.** sheaf

Review *don't* and *doesn't* on page 47 and other contractions from page 67 to 72.

7. Master the Contractions. Every language in the world uses short cuts. In English, short cuts are made by contracting — that is, by putting together and shortening words. In place of omitted letters is placed the apostrophe ('), probably the smallest and shortest punctuation mark.

Number your paper from 1-14. Beside each number, first write the original phrase, then the put-together form, then the shortened form using the apostrophe.

Example: 1. are not   arenot   aren't

1. was not	**8.** had not
2. were not	**9.** should not
3. do not	**10.** could not
4. does not	**11.** must not
5. did not	**12.** would not
6. has not	**13.** might not
7. have not	**14.** ought not

Watch out for these two exceptions.

can not   cannot   can't   will not   willnot   won't

Write ten sentences using any of the above contractions. Underline each contraction you use.

Here's another family of contractions. It presents problems because the shortened form *'ve* for *have* sounds like *of*. But everyone knows that *of* is a preposition, not a verb. Using *of* for *'ve* can make you look careless. This is the right way to form the contraction.

They have   Theyhave   They've

Number your paper from 1-9. Beside each number write the original phrase. Then run the words together. Finally shorten the phrase, substituting an apostrophe for the two missing letters.

1. you have	**4.** would have	**7.** might have
2. we have	**5.** could have	**8.** must have
3. I have	**6.** should have	**9.** may have

Write three sentences using at least one word from each column above. Underline each contraction.

In each set below, discover which letters should be omitted, and write the contractions.

I will   Iwill   I'll
they will

He has   hehas   he's
she has
Jim has

Jane is   Janeis   Jane's
here is
there is
who is
it is

I had   Ihad   I'd
you had
Bob has
he had
she had
we had
they had

you are   youare   you're
we are
they are
how are

Supply the contractions.

1. Can not you tell Jim tonight? He is planning to leave.
2. I did not know that.
3. He had better be notified soon or he will not go.
4. Maybe Bob has told him already.
5. I doubt that. It is unlike Bob to interfere.
6. Jane will be looking forward to seeing him.
7. Why are not you trying to get him now?
8. I should have brought my list of phone numbers.
9. Is not his number in the book?
10. Where is the phone book?

8. Study the Stumpers. Since only a few words present a spelling problem, studying the more difficult words will improve your spelling immensely. This is a list of some of the most used stumpers in English. Take one set a week. Have someone dictate them to you. Study those you miss by dividing them into syllables and concentrating on hard parts. Practice writing them until you can achieve a perfect list. Do not be satisfied to spell them aloud.

Writing and spelling orally are two entirely different skills. Once you've mastered one set, go on to the next. Occasionally return to words already mastered and at the end of the entire list, test yourself on all the words.

1	2	3	4	5
absence	apparent	cellar	develop	government
ache	article	column	different	guard
across	association	coming	disease	guess
actually	author	completely	divide	handsome
address	awful	country	doesn't	height
advertising	balance	defendant	eighth	hoping
all right	banana	definition	excellent	influence
always	before	dependent	February	innocence
among	breath	describe	forty	interest
answer	calendar	desperate	friend	knowledge

6	7	8	9	10
laboratory	naturally	perhaps	referred	tariff
laid	nephew	permanent	restaurant	temperature
library	niece	physical	rhythm	therefore
lonely	ninety	pleasant	safety	truly
magazine	ninth	practical	sandwich	Tuesday
marriage	omitted	probably	science	until
mathematics	operate	proceed	secretary	usually
meant	opportunity	quiet	several	vegetable
minute	parallel	really	similar	Wednesday
muscle	pastime	receive	succeed	writing

Words Are Power   pages 1-11

Through the lessons in this chapter you should

- be aware of some of the ways to expand vocabulary through context, through cultivation of special interests and through informed use of the dictionary

- be familiar with the various features within word entries as well as other information that dictionaries may contain

- be able to perform the following dictionary skills: locate words quickly
know how to find spelling, pronunciation, variant meanings, and synonyms.

P. 2   BE A SPECIALIST. The words in this exercise are related to witchcraft. Even though some of them may have other meanings, only those meanings connected with the specialized topic should be considered.

witch: a woman practicing the black arts
ceremoniously: using prescribed procedures
warlock: one given to black magic
eerie: frightening because of strangeness or gloominess
incantations: use of spells or verbal charms spoken or sung as part of a ritual of magic
poppet: doll, in this case probably used as an image of a hated person
amulet: a charm often inscribed with a magic incantation or symbol to protect the wearer against evil or to aid him
wizard: one skilled in magic, a sorcerer
cackling: laughing in a way suggestive of hen's cries after laying
forest: a track of woodland; legendary home of dark spirits

P. 3   WRITE A PARAGRAPH USING PICTURES. Some words you might incorporate into your paragraphs are:
ceramics, throw, kiln, potter's wheel, slip, horse show, riding habit, filly, equestrian, jockey, snow plow, goggles, skis, snow blind, snowmobile

P. 4   BE A DICTIONARY ADDICT. Unless you use a common source, your answers to the dictionary questions will vary. A variety of answers will show a wider range of information available. These are some possibilities:
Explanatory Notes, Guide to Pronunciation, Abbreviations Used in the Dictionary, Vocabulary of Abbreviations, Arbitrary Symbols and Proofreaders' Marks, Proof of Lincoln's Gettysburg Address, Biographical Names, Pronouncing Gazetteer, Forms of Address, Common English Names, Vocabulary of Rhymes, Spelling, Plurals, Punctuation, Compounds, Capitalization, Italicization, Colleges and Universities (U.S., Can.)

P. 4   ALPHABETICAL LIST astrodome, case, deep, gene, hoax, playback, rope, smoggy, undulation, zinnia

P. 5

A   courser, coursing, court, courteous, courtesan, courtesy

B   mask, medium, mist, moccasin, muddle, myrtle

C   radiate, realism, refine, roadster, rootless, rut

D   stickle, stickleback, stickler, stickman, stick out, stick pin

E   traitor, traitorous, traject, trajectory, tram, tramcar

UNSOUNDED LETTERS   psychedelic, pneumatic, knife, pharmacy, acquire, choir, ghost

P. 5   MISSPELLED WORDS   receive, cyanide, accident, psychology, carousel, yield, professor, fiery, (correct), allusion, all right, pasteurize, (correct), analyze, business, Messiah, scorching, eerie, drowned, kiln

Plurals   flies, men, data, monies, sheep, kinks, tours de force, kine, heroes

P. 6   PAST TENSE   controlled, sneaked, dived, dueled or duelled, swung, picnicked, might, froze, trod, could, broke, shredded

P. 6   PRIMARY AND SECONDARY ACCENTS
um brel'la, post'hu mous, per'fume,
per fume', per'fect, per fect',
im'po tent, ir'rev'o ca ble, af'flu'ence,
ad ver'tise ment', ad'mir a ble', com'ba tant',
fil let', fi na'le, ex'qui site',
in'fa mous, pen ta'me ter', mis'chie vous',
or o'gra phy, Yom'Kip'pur (Yom'Kip pur')

PP. 6–7   PRONUNCIATION
quay—me, calm—bomb, bade—lad, often—coffin, posterior—gospel, steppe—pep, data—late, respite—kit

P. 7   VARIANT MEANINGS   1. ⁴light 6a frivolous
2. ²light 2a not dark, intense or swarthy in color or coloring: PALE **3.** ¹light 3a: a celestial body **4.** ⁶light 1: DISMOUNT **5.** ⁴light 1d: containing less than the legal, standard or usual weight **6.** ¹light 8: something that enlightens or informs **7.** ¹light 6a public knowledge **8.** ¹light b DAWN **9.** ⁴light 3a easily disturbed **10.** ⁴light 13 DIZZY, GIDDY **11.** ⁴light 8 intended chiefly to entertain **12.** ⁴light 13 DIZZY GIDDY **13.** ⁶light—light into: to attack forcefully **14.** ⁴light 9a: having comparatively low alcoholic content **15.** ⁴light 2b exerting a minimum of force or pressure: faint

P. 10 VARIANT MEANINGS (TAKEN FROM WEBSTER'S 7TH) The following sentences are merely samples.

1. ¹throw 2a: to cause to fall
   He threw the switch.
2. ¹suite: 1: RETINUE, esp: the personal staff accompanying a ruler, diplomat or dignitary on official business.
   The suite was luxuriously spacious.
3. ¹dummy 6: a pattern arrangement of matter to be reproduced esp. by printing
   The dummy director made some brilliant changes in the film.
4. cauliflower ear: an ear deformed from injury and excessive growth of reparative tissue
   He likes his cauliflower with cheese sauce.
5. ¹board 4c: daily meals esp. when furnished for pay
   The board held a meeting to settle the pay scale.
6. ²rook to defraud by cheating or swindling
   Ludwig took the knight with his rook.
7. chameleon 2a: a fickle or changeable person
   The chameleon hid among the weeds.
8. ²throw ba: a light coverlet
   It's your throw, John.
9. ¹tight 10: intoxicated, drunk
   Scrooge was a tightwad.
10. ²sail(ed) 4: to attack something with gusto
    She sailed into the room gracefully, gliding from guest to guest on tiny satin slippers.
11. flummery 2: mummery, mumbo jumbo
    After surgery he was allowed nothing but flummery.
12. ¹jack 7 slang: money
    You need another jack to record in stereo.
13. ¹farm 6: a minor-league baseball club associated with a major-league club as a subsidiary to which recruits are assigned until needed or for further training
    The revenue from the neighboring farms subsidized the city's welfare program.
14. ²play 1b (1) to move aimlessly about: trifle
    Leave a few feet of rope free for play.
15. poke bonnet: a woman's bonnet with a projecting brim at the front
    Don't poke fun at him, Joe.

P. 10 SYNONYMS Sample sentences:
likely, reliable, credible, probably, promising, attractive
   You are likely to succeed if you try.
   The part looks promising for you.
predilection, prepossession, prejudice, bias
   His predilection for Beethoven stems from childhood exposure to the musical giant.
   Biased persons do not make good jurors.
serious, thoughtful, earnest, grave, solemn, sedate, staid, sober
   Please give the matter serious consideration.
   Risë Stevens assumed the role of a staid governess.
cure, rectify, remedy, heal

Will we ever find the cure for cancer?
The incision will heal in a few weeks.
end, termination, close, ending, terminus, death, destruction, remnant
   After seven long acts, the play ends tragically.
   The termination of the contract caused the manager to re-examine his methods.
native, inborn, innate, natural, indigenous, endemic, aboriginal
   His native talents were many.
   The aboriginals had their own code of honor.
taste, experience, undergo, test, flavor, savor, tang, relish, smack, gusto, palette
   Her exquisite taste was reflected in the subtle colors of the room.
   This pizza au passionata has a mouthwatering tang.
victory, conquest, triumph
   The victory came finally in the seventeenth inning.
   The dictator marched through the occupied city in triumph.
quick, prompt, ready, apt, live
   Get some tools and be quick about it!
   His ready answers amazed everyone.
oppose, combat, resist, withstand, antagonize
   Who will oppose the senator in the election?
   Can you withstand the pain without a drug?
fancy, taste, judgment, like, ornamental, extravagant, notion, whim, inclination
   Suddenly I have a fancy for a hot fudge sundae.
   The ornamental grillwork gave the mansion a Spanish flavor.
invent, fabricate, create, discovery
   Did you invent that alibi?
   It takes a lot of people-watching to create a moving drama.
cry, shout, weep, lament, slogan, proclamation
   A cry of "Fire!" echoed throughout the hotel.
   He wept at the death of his son.
irascible, choleric, splenetic, testy, touchy, cranky, cross
   The irascible widower shook his fist at the children running through his yard.
   The maid was cross at having to wash so many dishes.
join, combine, unite, connect, link, associate, relate
   He used glue to join the two pieces of wood.
   The minister united the couple in marriage.
kill, defeat, veto, slay, murder, assassinate, dispatch, execute, crush
   They had to kill all their diseased hogs.
   Caesar was assassinated on the Ides of March.
lack, want, need, require
   During the depression there was a lack of food.
   The barn wants painting.
juncture, pass, exigency, emergency, contingency, pinch, connection
   At that juncture, the board was all exhausted.
   The National Guard was called to meet the emergency.
unruly, ungovernable, intractable, refractory, recal-

citrant, willful, headstrong
> The teacher was successful in subduing the unruly child.
> The delinquent had a recalcitrant attitude.

erase, expunge, cancel, efface, obliterate, blot (out), delete
> No need to erase with Ko-rec-Type.
> Delete his name from the list.

P. 11   IDENTIFY THE MISFIT.   1. island **2.** breathed **3.** jumped **4.** substantial **5.** grate

P. 11   WHICH WORDS?   1. recent **2.** contemporary **3.** fresh **4.** new **1.** shuffled **2.** strode **3.** scurried **4.** ambled **1.** tall **2.** lanky **3.** big **4.** gigantic

P. 11   PICK THE BEST WORD.   1. vigorous **2.** blooming **3.** healthy **4.** flourishing **5.** thriving

Language That Counts   pages 12–33

After doing the lessons in the chapter, you should

- be able to recognize simple subjects and predicates, nouns, verbs, adverbs and adjectives
- be able to write original subjects and predicates
- use articles correctly, form noun inflections and capitalize proper nouns
- correctly form regular verb inflections: simple form, third person singular, -ed and ing forms
- correctly form the past tense of irregular verbs
- use adverbs and adjectives.

P. 13   WRITE A PREDICATE.   Answers will vary.

P. 13   SUPPLY A SUBJECT.   Answers will vary.

PP. 14–15   SUPPLY SUBJECT OR PREDICATE.   1. hurried P **2.** Shepherd S **3.** Lem (he) S **4.** arrived P **5.** whispered P **6.** read P **7.** Have ___ read P **8.** I S **9.** wrote P **10.** I S

P. 16   SUPPLY *A* OR *AN* BEFORE NOUNS.   a horse, an umbrella, a bush, an hour, an apple, an emerald, an igloo, a hospital, a picnic, a radio, a xylophone, an acid, an aging cat, a stocking, a camera, an old camera, a new radio, a pair of stockings, a holey stocking, an honest man

P. 16   WRITE SENTENCES.   Answers will vary.

P. 16   WRITE THE PLURALS.   wishes, words, searches, earphones, voyages, trips, axes, plays, plants, itches

P. 17   MAKE THE NOUNS POSSESSIVE.   child's cat, cats' paws, books' bindings, plant's leaves, teacher's shoes, telephone's ring, animals' skins, elephant's tusk, Ray's glasses, Smiths' house

P. 17   DETERMINERS   1. zero determiner, zero determiner, zero determiner **2.** zero determiner or the, the **3.** the **4.** zero determiner **5.** zero determiner, zero determiner

P. 17   IDENTIFY THE NOUNS IN THE PHOTOGRAPHS.   Some nouns that might be listed are the following:
streetlight, man, woman, car, tree, building, fountain.

P. 18   WRITE A SENTENCE WITH NOUNS.   The following are not nouns:
3. Hello **14.** of **15.** since **16.** beautiful

P. 18   IDENTIFY THE NOUNS   The determiners and nouns are: zero, Jack, S; the, side, S; the, house, S; The, wind, S; the, leaves, P; a, ledge, S; his, balance, S; his, eyes, P; the, frame, S; his, back, S; his, feet, P; the, air, S

P. 18   COMMON AND PROPER NOUNS   1. Cleveland **2.** Susan **3.** Halloween **4.** Mount Fuji **5.** Colonel Sanders **6.** Singer

P. 18   REVIEW   burst, paid, left

P. 19   FIND THE PREDICATE   1. walked **2.** leaned **3.** want **4.** said **5.** jumped

PP. 21–22   SELECT A FORM.   1. used **2.** called **3.** added **4.** moved **5.** supposed **6.** cries **7.** drowned **8.** furnished **9.** knocked **10.** pitches **11.** obeyed **12.** attacked **13.** knits (knitted) **14.** tries **15.** turned (turn) **16.** iron (ironed) **17.** bathes **18.** prejudice **19.** bomb (bombed) **20.** squealed **21.** dined **22.** wrapped **23.** echoes (echoed) **24.** dived (dives) **25.** jumped (jump) **26.** sneaked **27.** decayed **28.** hurried **29.** judged **30.** taxed (taxes) **31.** talked **32.** noticed

PP. 22–23   EXERCISES 1–5   Sentences will vary.

P. 23   Sentences will vary, but the verb form should be:
1. offered, obeyed, dined, tried, stopped, supposed, used, drowned, knocked, bathed, prejudiced
2. drowns, dives, attacks, argues, squeals, wraps, taxes, prejudices, measures
3. is turning, is using, is sneaking, is performing, is hurrying, is jumping, is dining, is crying, is attacking
4. stays, turns, uses, wraps, bathes, hurries, furnishes, flows, echoes, drowns
5. performs, acts, adds, attaches, moves, irons, furnishes, uses, turns

P. 24   CORRECT THE VERB FORM. (STRESS SPELLING.)   occurred, offered, dives, diving, argued, judges, stayed, stepped, were knocking (knocked), sneaked, jumped, turned, realized, drowned, stayed, suppose, clutched, dragged

P. 24   FORM THE REGULAR VERBS BY ADDING -S OR -ES.   1. lies 2. issues 3. anoints 4. accepts 5. appears 6. taxes 7. poisons 8. wishes 9. asks 10. drags

P. 24   ADD -ED TO SIMPLE VERBS   1. tossed 2. uttered 3. played 4. hailed 5. deserted 6. skated 7. hanged 8. controlled 9. profited 10. proceeded

P. 25   ADD -ING TO SIMPLE VERBS.   1. deceiving 2. compelling 3. tackling 4. succeeding 5. bouncing 6. rhyming 7. transferring 8. receiving 9. arriving 10. skimming

P. 25   COMPLETE THE SENTENCES.   Suggested answers.
1. lured 2. wandered, were budding 3. attracted 4. confronted, passed 5. noticed, were hiding 6. grew 7. clustered 8. experienced 9. recognized 10. greeted, commented

PP. 26–27   IRREGULAR VERBS   1. cost 2. cut 3. quit 4. read 5. slit 6. cut 7. put 8. burst 9. hurts 10. thrust

P. 27   PAST FORMS   1. drank 2. broke 3. bought 4. drove 5. blew 6. brought 7. came, brought 8. broke 9. did 10. began

PP. 27–28   WRITE SENTENCES USING PAST TENSE.   Answers will vary.

P. 28   SUPPLY THE PAST FORM.   1. ate 2. led 3. flew 4. fell 5. hung 6. knew 7. got 8. gave 9. froze 10. went

P. 28   WRITE SENTENCES USING PAST TENSE.   Answers will vary.

P. 28   SUPPLY THE PAST FORM.   1. saw 2. left 3. paid 4. lay 5. ran 6. rode 7. rang 8. rose 9. lost 10. said

P. 29   WRITE SENTENCES USING THE PAST TENSE.   Answers will vary.

P. 29   SUPPLY THE PAST FORM   1. woke, wrote 2. swung 3. wrung 4. shrank 5. thought 6. spoke 7. stole 8. threw 9. shot 10. took

PP. 29–30   CHOOSE A SUITABLE FORM OF THE VERB.   1. drinks 2. saw 3. stole 4. lay 5. blew 6. lost 7. takes 8. wrung 9. wrote 10. rose 11. led 12. knew 13. broke 14. came 15. gives, gave 16. went 17. flew 18. brought 19. swung 20. shrank

P. 30   WRITE THE RIGHT FORM.   1. taught 2. told 3. hid 4. sold 5. dealt 6. bled 7. bade 8. flung 9. clung 10. lent 11. slid 12. sank 13. slew 14. sat 15. sang 16. strung 17. won 18. wore 19. tore 20. swept

PP. 30–31   PUT THE CORRECT FORM INTO THE SLOTS.   1. met 2. became 3. bent 4. bought 5. fell 6. fled 7. ground 8. left 9. began 10. meant

P. 31   THE LATEST THING   How is the "Rimed Grammar" different from your grammar and language lessons?
1. Definitions are not all inclusive. A noun is the name of a person, place, idea or thing, not only of a thing. Being verbs are not included in the definition. Adverbs tell how, when, where and to what extent.
2. Definitions exemplify the parts of speech for identification whereas the *Basic Grammar Guides* teach them through use.
Memorizing these labels may be a helpful learning device.

P. 32   FIND THE "HOW" ADVERBS.   1. noisily 2. graciously 3. With a flourish 4. hungrily 5. with such a straight face

PP. 32–33   LOCATE THE ADVERB OR ADVERBIAL PHRASE AND TELL WHAT QUESTION IT ANSWERS.   1. to sea (where) 2. on his knees (where) 3. by boat (how) 4. home (where), until February (when) 5. very (to what extent) 6. on the tuffet (where) 7. Because of the spider (why), in a hurry (how) 8. to school (where) 9. with a limp (how) 10. loudly (how), outside the classroom (where) 11. away (where), together (how)

P. 33   FIND ALL THE ADJECTIVES   1. gray, old, striped, beautiful, pea-green 2. nasty, poor, high 3. good, little 4. unkind 5. pretty, young

Structures   pages 34–40

After doing the lessons in this chapter, you should

• recognize transitive verbs and their direct objects, intransitive verbs, linking verbs, predicate complements whether noun, adjective or adverb

• be able to write original sentences using these structures

• be able to use concrete sense words.

P. 34   INTRODUCTION   The buildings shown are: the brownstone in which Theodore Roosevelt was born
a villa in Switzerland
Federal Hall National Memorial

P. 36   IDENTIFY THE DIRECT OBJECT.   1. tune 2. tune 3. tune 4. girl 5. mosquito 6. baton 7. hole 8. curtains 9. painting 10. men

P. 37   IDENTIFY VI. AND VT. AS WELL AS OBJECTS.   1. stirs vt., deal 2. practice vi. 3. polish vt., speeches, delivery 4. coach vt., them 5. choose vt., experts 6. arrives vi. 7. is vi. 8. perform vi. 9. quake and tremble vi. 10. choose vt., speakers

P. 38   FIND LINKING VERB AND PREDICATE NOUN OR PREDICATE ADJECTIVE.   1. is, adj.

(overweight) **2.** is, adj. (broken) **3.** is, n. (boy) **4.** is, adj. (slippery) **5.** is, n. (fruit) **6.** are, adj. (cheap) **7.** be followed by adverb (here) **8.** is, adj. (nourishing) **9.** was, n. (liquids) **10.** was, adj. (trembling) **11.** has been, adj. (sick) **12.** has been, n. (manager) **13.** had been, adj. (sickly) **14.** were, adj. (cheap) **15.** are, adj. (easy) **16.** be followed by adverb (at the play) **17.** is, n. (o'clock) **18.** might be, adj. (tight) **19.** could be, n. (end) **20.** might have been, n. (star)

P. 39   IDENTIFY LINKING VERB AND PREDI-CATE NOUN OR PREDICATE ADJECTIVE.   1. is, n. (person) **2.** seems, adj. (elated) **3.** non-linking verb **4.** is, adj. (better) **5.** appears, adj. (stable) **6.** were, adj. (contented) **7.** was, adj. (sure) **8.** was, n. (servant) **9.** was, adj. (capable) **10.** is, n. (dollars)

P. 40   SUBSTITUTE A LINKING VERB FOR EQUAL SIGN.   Answers are merely suggestive. **1.** looks **2.** is **3.** am **4.** are **5.** was **6.** seemed **7.** were **8.** appears **9.** am **10.** is

P. 45   WRITE A SENTENCE FOR EACH PIC-TURE.   Some descriptive words that might follow the linking verbs are:
sounds: harmonious, rhythmic, loud, soft
smells: savory, tantalizing, pungent, inviting
looks: thoughtful, pensive, interested, curious

Working Together   pages 41–58

After completing the lessons in this chapter, you should

- recognize
  singular and plural forms of nouns and verbs
  elements of a prepositional phrase
  indefinite pronouns
  the difference between simple and compound subjects and predicates
  fragments formed by mistaking prepositional and -ing phrases for sentences
  compound sentences joined by coordinate conjunctions
- be able to achieve agreement in number between
  simple subject and simple predicate
  indefinite pronouns and predicate despite or in accord with intervening prepositional phrase
  forms of do and predicate
  compound subjects and predicate
- edit sentences to incorporate phrase fragments and correct runovers
- write original sentences employing forms of do and combining brief sentences into compound sentences.

P. 42   TELL WHETHER SINGULAR OR PLURAL.   1. S **2.** P **3.** S **4.** S **5.** S **6.** S **7.** either S or P

8. P **9.** S **10.** S **11.** S **12.** either S or P **13.** P **14.** P **15.** S **16.** P **17.** S **18.** S **19.** S **20.** P

P. 42   DECIDE AGREEMENT.   1. C **2.** X **3.** X **4.** C **5.** C **6.** X **7.** X **8.** X **9.** C **10.** X **11.** X **12.** X **13.** X **14.** C **15.** X **16.** X **17.** C **18.** C **19.** X **20.** C

P. 43   SUPPLY CORRECT VERB FORM.   1. sings **2.** sing **3.** sing **4.** dance **5.** cook **6.** like **7.** prefers **8.** does **9.** is **10.** are

P. 43   CHOOSE THE -S OR SIMPLE FORM.   1. need **2.** require **3.** files **4.** is **5.** is **6.** frightens **7.** turn **8.** Has **9.** Does **10.** includes

PP. 43–44   SUPPLY THE SENSIBLE FORM.   1. have **2.** has, have **3.** are **4.** does **5.** are **6.** have **7.** am **8.** has **9.** Do **10.** Are

P. 45   FIND THE PREPOSITIONAL PHRASES IN THIS PARAGRAPH.   In winter, about taking trips [or sailing], to Florida, around the world, on a banana boat, to you, at times, of studying, Between December and April, up to my ears, in papers, into bed, for months

P. 46   CHOOSE THE RIGHT VERB.   1. Does **2.** want **3.** is **4.** likes **5.** was **6.** were **7.** does **8.** pitch **9.** were **10.** remains

1. seems **2.** has **3.** have **4.** have **5.** become

P. 47   TOP   1. is **2.** Does **3.** gets **4.** is **5.** have **6.** goes **7.** have **8.** volunteers **9.** Does **10.** begins

P. 47   WRITE THE CORRECT VERB.   1. don't **2.** don't **3.** don't **4.** doesn't **5.** doesn't **6.** don't **7.** doesn't **8.** doesn't **9.** don't **10.** doesn't

P. 47   WRITE SENTENCES.   Sentences will vary.

P. 48   REVIEW   1. enjoy **2.** have **3.** don't **4.** doesn't **5.** are **6.** is **7.** prefers **8.** are **9.** were **10.** were **11.** moves **12.** takes **13.** refuse **14.** does **15.** watch **16.** do **17.** helps **18.** am, is **19.** watches **20.** needs **21.** is **22.** wants **23.** gets **24.** does **25.** is **26.** likes

P. 50   FIND THE COMPOUNDS   1. Kenneth and Mel **2.** no compounds **3.** turned, spotted, and ran **4.** Ken and Mel **5.** gave up, and turned

P. 50   FIND THE COMPOUNDS.   1. curtains or drapes **2.** fusses or screams **3.** neither paint nor wallpaper **4.** fish or cut **5.** either go or join **6.** neither Mary nor Margaret **7.** either clever or lucky

P. 51   SUPPLY THE NEEDED VERB.   1. are **2.** was **3.** are **4.** are **5.** takes off **6.** do **7.** is **8.** begins **9.** is **10.** are

PP. 51–52   WRITE THE SINGULAR OR PLURAL VERB.   1. is **2.** are **3.** produce **4.** have **5.** lead **6.** sell **7.** is **8.** is **9.** pay **10.** do

P. 52 DIVIDE THE SENTENCES INTO COMPLETE SUBJECT AND PREDICATE.

1. The baby / took her first step today.
2. She / [With a little glue] repaired the broken vase.
3. A musty and soiled washcloth / hung over the greasy sink.
4. Miss Bumbry / sang the aria with perfect ease.
5. The withered and arthritic old man / sneezed painfully.
6. Sirius / is the brightest star in Orion.
7. A parsec / is equal to 3.26 light years.
8. White dwarfs / are about one million times denser than the sun.
9. The bride / tripped on the step and sprawled before the minister.
10. Her horrified groom and the nervous best man / laughed helplessly.

P. 53 FIND THE FRAGMENTS AND ADD THEM TO THE COMPLETE SENTENCE. Note: The position of the addition is merely suggested.

1. If you love horses, you can be a trainer *or a vet.*
2. Or, *like other prize-winning equestrians,* you can ride until you're good enough to jump.
3. *A good coach* and plenty of experience and time in the saddle are important.
4. You have to take riding seriously *to spend three hours everyday in the saddle.*
5. You've got to work up a positive relationship with your horse who must respond to you completely, *but not sense your nervousness.*

PP. 53–54 REWRITE THESE SENTENCES INCORPORATING FRAGMENTS.

1. Listening to the radio every morning and evening, the lonely child found some recreation.
2. Starting up the ignition with a grunt, snort and scrape, Phil rubbed his leather gloves together with satisfaction.
3. Freezing the ice cream and keeping it frozen were the challenges of the busy ice cream stand.
4. Practicing almost incessantly on the drum for three months, he drove all the neighbors wild.
5. Settling for a scrap of food and a dirty coat, the beggar turned away disappointed.

P. 54 MAKE UP YOUR OWN SENTENCES. Answers will vary.

PP. 54–55 IDENTIFY COMPLETE SENTENCES AND FRAGMENTS AND COMBINE INTO INTEGRATED SENTENCES.

1. S - frag Dogs and cats should engage in several activities, a little running, a little playing, a little hunting and a little sleeping.
2. frag - S But eating is the most enjoyable activity of all.
3. S - frag You have to consider three things: nutrition, appetite and your budget.
4. frag - S Coming in three basic types, complete cat and dog foods are available in dry, semi-moist and moist form.
5. frag - S Sold in bags from one to fifty pounds, dog food is least expensive.
6. S - frag The middle price range is composed of one-serving packets of semi-moist consistency.
7. frag - S Finally, the canned foods are most expensive.
8. S - frag Reward your pet now and then with special treat foods in cans or biscuits.
9. S - frag Some dogs stay on one food they're trained to for life.
10. frag - S Turning up their noses and rejecting what you've fed them for years, cats are more unpredictable.
11. S - frag Almost everyone was rescued from the burning house, all but Peterson.
12. frag - S Not a cent, not one red cent will I leave to that no-good grandson.
13. frag - S Stealing noiselessly into the house, he was surprised to find his father at the top of the stairs.
14. S - frag Houses in California are made of sturdy materials, such as concrete and stucco.
15. S - frag Following the dog's muddy tracks, they found him cowering in a corner, aware of his misdeeds.

P. 55 REWRITE THE FOLLOWING PARAGRAPHS CORRECTING FRAGMENTS.

1. You'll enjoy shopping by mail. You can see all the items available at a glance. You can take your good old time making a decision. And best of all, the mailman is the only one who will end up with sore feet.

2. But there are some disadvantages to mail order or phone shopping. You can't actually see the product. You may choose something unfit, or not as glamorous as on the ad page. Then too, it isn't always wise to send money ahead especially to unfamiliar mail order companies.

3. When you do order something by mail, identify your order completely. This may sound silly, but some people forget important information like their name and address. Keep a copy of your order together with the name and address of the company and the date. Paying by money order or check and including tax, shipping and postage costs, you'll save yourself a lot of headaches.

P. 56 MAKE THE FOLLOWING INTO LEGITIMATE COMPOUND SENTENCES.

1. Some people tend to be "day" people, for they easily snap to it before sunrise.
2. Early birds are often finished after dinner or near four, and they don't wake up again till sunrise.
3. Others find it hard to rise, and they do not find it easy to be cheerful till after dinner.
4. They are the life of the party beginning at five in the afternoon, and they are still raring to go at two in the morning.

5. Some people include a bit of both, for they may have two low and two high points a day.
6. Plants and animals are equipped with biological calendars, and humans are too.
7. Daily cycles ebb and flow in rhythms, for body temperature, blood pressure, blood sugar, breathing and pulse rate vary around a day.
8. These rhythms operate on a rough cycle of 24 hours, and they are probably inherited.
9. The story of human rhythms is a new field, but there have always been people who understood the human time sense.
10. People cannot expect to do their best work when body temperature is at its lowest, nor can they expect to sleep when body temperature is highest.

P. 57   TELL WHETHER SENTENCES ARE COMPOUND. 1. C 2. X 3. C 4. X 5. C 6. X 7. X 8. X 9. C 10. X

PP. 57–58   REWRITE THE FOLLOWING PARAGRAPHS CORRECTING COMMA FAULTS.
1.   You can cover 350 square feet of wall or ceiling with a gallon of paint. First you'll need to cover floors and furniture with drop cloths. You can buy inexpensive pieces of plastic or you can use old sheets or large pieces of canvas. Next you should remove all light switch and wall plug plates. Then you should cover baseboards, and window frame edges with masking tape. Filling in plastic cracks and holes with spackling compound is the next step. When it is dry you can sand it smooth.
2.   Like people, paint prefers weather that is in-between, not too hot and not too cold. Rainy days are also bad. To prevent splattering and dripping, you should dip your brush into the paint only one third the length of the bristles. The order is woodwork first, ceiling next, and finally the walls. You can begin at the upper left hand corner of a wall, working toward the floor in a narrow strip. Painting two-foot strips just below the ceiling line is the next step. Then you can finish the wall.
3.   At the baseboard you can use a brush for areas the roller couldn't reach. You'll want to wipe up spills and splatters or drips immediately because it is harder to get dry paint off. Above all, at the end, you should save paint and brushes. Tightly replace the lid on the paint can and clean brushes and roller to save money. You should know that paint looks deeper and darker on a wall than on the sample color card.

Sound-Alikes   pages 59–73

After completing the lessons in this chapter, you should

• have a mastery of the meaning and spelling of basic homonyms, especially the troublesome words: your, there, its, whose and to.

• be able to originate sentences using the homonyms correctly

P. 60   GROUP ONE   1. brakes **2.** blue **3.** blew **4.** allowed **5.** bare **6.** breaks **7.** bear

P. 61   GROUP TWO   by, canvas, board, sell, course, scent, buy, coarse, sent, canvass, cent

P. 61   GROUP THREE   fare, fair, four, dear, for, flour, flower, dessert, deserted, for

P. 62   GROUP FOUR   Possibilities for the pictured words: herd, hour, hole

P. 63   GROUP FIVE   night, led, loose, lose, no, knew, know, no, lead, new

PP. 63–64   GROUP SIX   maid, male, meat, meet, one, won, mail, pale, made, meet

P. 64   GROUP SEVEN   principal, plane, plain, passed, pared, peace, principal

P. 65   GROUP EIGHT   rap, quiet, ring, rain, wring, quite, ring, wrap, rite, write

P. 66   GROUP NINE   shone, rode, road, see, sea, sight, rowed, site, sale

P. 66   GROUP TEN   1. Some, stationery **2.** stealing, some **3.** steel **4.** son, tail **5.** tale, sun

P. 67   MAKE A CHOICE.   1. bear, bare **2.** heal, heel **3.** pare, pear **4.** reign, rain **5.** site **6.** ate, eight **7.** bored, board **8.** meet, meat **9.** read, Red **10.** ring, wring **11.** rowed, rode, road **12.** quiet **13.** pair **14.** rein

PP. 67–68   TROUBLE WORDS   1. your **2.** your **3.** your **4.** You're **5.** Your **6.** You're **7.** Your **8.** You're **9.** your **10.** your

P. 68   THE LATEST THING   Strange words: ere (archaic, poetic); eyre (English History); aught (archaic, "to any degree"); awn (standard); auln (obsolete); barb (standard); barbe (obsolete); bate (archaic, "to deprive of"); baize (standard); bays (obsolete); gravest (last definition where it means "lowest part")

P. 69   CHOOSE THERE, THEIR, OR THEY'RE.   1. their **2.** their **3.** there **4.** There **5.** there **6.** they're **7.** There **8.** there **9.** They're, their **10.** they're

P. 69   WHICH FORM?   1. it's **2.** its **3.** it's **4.** It's **5.** it's **6.** Its **7.** it's **8.** it's **9.** It's **10.** Its

P. 70   ANOTHER PAIR OF HOMONYMS   1. who's **2.** whose **3.** whose **4.** who's **5.** whose **6.** who's **7.** who's **8.** who's **9.** whose **10.** who's

P. 70   1. to **2.** too, to **3.** Two **4.** too **5.** to **6.** to, too **7.**

Two **8.** too **9.** to **10.** to, two **11.** too **12.** to **13.** two **14.** To **15.** too

P. 71 REVIEW TROUBLE WORDS. 1. It's **2.** whose **3.** There **4.** your, your **5.** their **6.** too **7.** your **8.** It's, you're too **9.** your **10.** there **11.** It's **12.** your **13.** It's **14.** It's, too **15.** its **16.** They're **17.** there **18.** to **19.** whose **20.** You're **21.** Who's **22.** You're **23.** too **24.** There **25.** two

PP. 71–72 TWELVE TROUBLE WORDS 1. yours (theirs) **2.** too, to **3.** to **4.** You're **5.** their **6.** their, your **7.** too **8.** you're **9.** too **10.** It's **11.** Whose **12.** your **13.** You're **14.** It's **15.** you're **16.** to, their **17.** Who's **18.** too, to **19.** you're **20.** its **21.** your **22.** Who's **23.** You're **24.** your **25.** It's

P. 72 PROOFREAD. With its ears hanging low and its tail between its legs, the mongrel flopped after the children. In obedience to their mother, they shooed the dog away, but their commands were only half-hearted. They knew it didn't belong to any of their friends. They wondered whose dog he was. The dog's actions showed that he knew their real desires. Ever since they'd lost Ricky, who had to be put to sleep after the mower's blade cut off his ear, the children envied everyone else's dogs. For two cents they would have carried this mutt home with them now, but their mother's warning sounded in their ears: "I don't care whose dog he was. You're not bringing any dogs into this house." And so they chased him away while half inviting him to stay.

P. 73 WRITE AN ORIGINAL PARAGRAPH ABOUT THIS SCENE. Some possessives might include: farmer's hat, his boots, calf's mother, cow's bell, her calf, whose shirt, its hide.

How to Capitalize All the Words in the English Language with Style and Sincerity and Do It Right   pages 74–87

After working the exercises in this chapter, you should

- be familiar with the two main rules for capitalization: beginnings and proper nouns
- be able to apply the capitalization rules for beginnings
  I, O
  the first word of every complete sentence
  the first word of every complete sentence of a direct quote
  the first word of the salutation and complimentary close of a letter
- recognize the difference between common and proper nouns
- be able to apply the rules for proper nouns
  names of particular persons, places, things and ideas

persons
places: addresses
ideas: specific eras, historical events, special events, calendar events, special identities, business and political events and organizations
things: specific vehicles, trade names.

P. 75 FIND THE WORDS 1. I **2.** none **3.** I'll **4.** I, O **5.** I

P. 75 SUPPLY CAPITALS. dog. Actually . . . him. Why . . . she? She . . . him. His . . . too. She . . . daily. Practically . . . her. No

P. 75 WHICH WORDS SHOULD BE CAPITALIZED? 1. New It **2.** Many **3.** Some **4.** fragment **5.** Beyond **6.** Hotels **7.** Restaurants **8.** Still **9.** Every **10.** For

PP. 76–77 SUPPLY THE CAPITALS NEEDED. 1. "Can't **2.** "The **3.** "So, You're **4.** none **5.** "It's **6.** none **7.** "Do, "It

P. 77 SUPPLY THE CAPITALS. 1. Sincerely **2.** My **3.** Dear **4.** Your **5.** My, Grandmother **6.** Your **7.** Your **8.** none **9.** Very **10.** Gratefully

P. 77 REWRITE THE LETTER. My, O, Wouldn't, I've, Yes, I'm, I, Suddenly, I, "Mom," I, Then, To, I, I, Needless, Reading, I'm, I. Don't, Your

P. 78 PARTICULAR NOUNS Public School #1, Northwest Territory, Jordan River, Declaration of Independence, Old Hickory, Governor Alfred E. Smith, Saturday, The *Times*, Marsha Jones, Twin Towers, Blippo, England, the West, Bible, Dan Jacobs, *The Turn of the Screw*, Geography I, February, Mars, Chinese, Coach Machock, Jim Machock

P. 81 ENVELOPE ADDRESSES
1. 2743 Scranton Road
   Beldon, California
2. 11545 Heath Road, North
   Chesterland, Ohio
3. 85 East Seventh Street
   Berlin, Massachusetts
4. 116 Belvedere Boulevard
   Saxon, Virginia
5. 36 Hampton Square, Apt. #6
   Sidney, New Jersey
6. 4511 Wetzel Place
   Johnston, Pennsylvania
7. 4503 Lakeland Court
   Annandale, Tennessee
8. 23685 Dixie Highway
   Fairfax, Kentucky
9. P. O. Box 400
   New York, New York
10. 850 Caxton Building
    Rochester, New York

P. 81   COPY THE CORRECT FORM.   1. a. Northwest Territory **2.** a. Go south till you see a church **3.** Fifty-first Street **4.** b. the Brooklyn Bridge **5.** b. the Great Western Divide **6.** a. Strait of Gibraltar **7.** a. Mount Everest **8.** b. Ohio State Penitentiary **9.** a. Rocky Mountain National Park **10.** b. Virginia Beach

P. 82   CORRECTLY CAPITALIZE.   1. Women's Amateur Golf Match **2.** World War II **3.** the World Series **4.** Counter-Reformation **5.** New Stone Age **6.** Chicago Fire **7.** Modern Age **8.** Battle of Wounded Knee **9.** Nascar Grand National Races **10.** the Winter Olympics **11.** Spanish-American War **12.** Battle of Lexington **13.** War of the Roses **14.** French Revolution **15.** Industrial Age **16.** Contemporary Period **17.** World Food Conference **18.** Romantic Age **19.** Dark Ages **20.** Kentucky Derby

PP. 82–83   WHICH WORDS CAPITALIZED?   New Year's Day, February, Lincoln's and Washington's Birthdays
Ground Hog Day, Valentine's Day, March, Lent, Ash Wednesday, February, April, Easter
Passover, March, St. Patrick's Day, May, Memorial Day

P. 83   WRITE WORDS TO BE CAPITALIZED IN THE PARAGRAPH.   World Conference of Peoples, European, English, French, German, Greek, Italian, Portuguese, Dutch, Danish, Flemish, Norwegian, Finnish, Swiss, Spanish, Polish, Slovak, Slovenian, Czech, Hungarian
Middle East, Arabic, Hebrew, Lebanese, Turkish, Persian
South Asia, Hindi, Urdu, Malay, Bengali
Southeast Asia, Vietnamese, Burmese, Sudanese, Pidgin English, Indonesian, Javanese, Balinese
Far East, Chinese, Nepali, Japanese, Korean, Mongolian, Tibetan
Negroid, Mongoloid, Caucasoid
Christian, Roman Catholic, Eastern Orthodox, Protestant
Jewish, Moslem, Zoroastrian, Shinto, Taoist, Confucian, Buddhist, Hindu

P. 84   SUPPLY THE NEEDED CAPITALS.
1. Republicans, Senate, Congress, Supreme Court, Republican, Cabinet, Republican, Democratic
2. Student Council, Spanish Club Entertainment Committee, Hess Pharmacy, Thoreau High School

P. 85   WRITE THE WORDS.   Russians, Sixties, Vostok I, Vostok II, Mercury Atlas 6, Vostok III and IV, Mercury Atlas 8 and 9, Gemini, Soyuz 1, Soyuz, Apollo, Russian, American

PP. 85–86   INSERT CAPITALS.
1. Asia, Australia, Malayan, Papuan, Chinese, Bahasa Indonesian, Malay, English
2. Moslem, Indonesians, Christian, Bali, Buddhist, Hindu, Malaysian, Portuguese, Australian
3. United States, Republican, Democrats, Federalist, Democratic-Republican, Whig

P. 86   WRITE THE CAPITALS.   1. Adirondack Mountains **2.** Dumont-Durville High School **3.** Darius the Great **4.** Puget Sound **5.** Washington, D.C. **6.** Ohio-Allegheny River **7.** the Great Lakes **8.** the Language Department **9.** The Gulf of Mexico **10.** Harvard University **11.** west of the Rockies **12.** Laurentian Plain **13.** Central Plateau **14.** Arctic Slope **15.** House of Representatives **16.** St. Theresa Academy **17.** correct **18.** the Gunpowder Plot **19.** Great Dane **20.** Correct **21.** Room **22.** Correct **23.** Kennedy Freeway **24.** Salt Lake City, Utah **25.** General Motors **26.** Civil War Period **27.** Lorain County **28.** un-American

PP. 86–87   SEARCH OUT WORDS.
1. Fathers, Declaration of Independence, Congress, American Revolution, Philadelphia, Washington, D.C.
2. Jane Addams High School, Abbeville, Georgia, Typing III, Advanced Stenography, Business Law
3. Tang, Kellogg's Rice Krispies, Wonder, Swift's
4. First National Bank Building, Masonic Auditorium, Ely Estate, Superior, Thirty-fifth Street
5. Ambassador, Wednesday, July 7, Tuesday, July 12, Boeing, Chicago, Illinois, Pontiac
6. Russian, American, Taurus I, Mars
7. Ohio Turnpike, Route 57, Cascade Bridge, Black River, Oberlin Road
8. February 2, Groundhog's Day
9. Irish, Italian, German
10. Democrats, Republicans, Appalachian, Tennessee

Put Your Mark on It   pages 88–97

At the end of the chapter you should understand the importance of punctuation for conveying meaning and

- be able to apply the end marks: periods, question marks, exclamation points
- understand and know how to use commas to
  separate items in addresses and dates
  follow the salutation and complimentary close of a friendly letter
  separate similar items of a series
  separate adjectives preceding a noun
  set off introductory elements, items in direct address
- be able to originate sentences using these marks of punctuation.

P. 90   IDENTIFY DIRECT QUESTIONS AND REWRITE OTHERS.
1. How does he like his steak?
2. Does he like it rare?
3. Is Jack a good cook?
4. Will you hold the candle while I light it?
5. When is the steak coming?

PP. 90–91 SUPPLY END MARKS. (Exclamation points may vary according to individual interpretation.) **1.** wind. **2.** Bill. **3.** hand? **4.** me. **5.** sailboat. **6.** (fragment) **7.** way. **8.** Lou! balance! **9.** west! **10.** quits? **11.** advice. **12.** that? **13.** (fragment) **14.** now. you. **15.** can. or (!) **16.** do? **17.** can. **18.** want? **19.** it. **20.** Quick! Ease . . . rope. **21.** shore. **22.** Lou, Lou! The . . . way! **23.** chance. **24.** Bill. **25.** Lou. **26.** again. **27.** came?

P. 91 SUPPLY END MARKS. Help! Thief! shoe! seat. here. shoe. them. Ouch! oaf! side. shiny.

P. 91 THE LATEST THING Marks used only in a printed book: index, section, obelisk, double dagger, paragraph.

P. 92 WRITE THE WORDS THAT SHOULD BE FOLLOWED BY COMMAS. 1. Saginaw, Michigan, **2.** Greenfield, Illinois, **3.** Avenue, Berkley, **4.** none, **5.** London, England,

P. 92 WHERE DO COMMAS BELONG? 1. 12, 1906, **2.** 13, 1998, **3.** none **4.** Saturday, 15, **5.** none

P. 93 COMMAS FOR SHORT ITEMS 1. mischief, (salutation) **2.** Tuesday, October 31, **3.** no comma **4.** Washington, D.C., **5.** Chicago, Illinois, **6.** Oberlin, Ohio, **7.** Road, New Haven, **8.** yours, **9.** Dolly, **10.** no comma, **11.** no comma **12.** no comma **13.** 15, 1875, **14.** no comma, **15.** 14, 1789, **16.** Paris, **17.** Cambridge, Ohio, **18.** Scottsbluff, Nebraska, **19.** Cairo, Illinois, **20.** Winesburg, Ohio,

P. 94 SERIES COMMAS (The comma before the final conjunction is optional.) **1.** dough, sauce, cheese, **2.** water, **3.** stewed, baked, **4.** Carefully, **5.** hissed, rattled, **6.** humiliated, lonely, **7.** Quietly, cautiously, **8.** none **9.** whistled, stamped

PP. 94–95 ADJECTIVES IN A SERIES 1. shiny, **2.** big, **3.** none **4.** Big, **5.** deep,

P. 95 WORDS TO BE FOLLOWED BY COMMAS (The comma before the final conjunction is optional.) **1.** no comma **2.** pickles, relish, **3.** no comma **4.** Slowly, **5.** tough, **6.** hit, **7.** no comma **8.** blocking, kicking, **9.** no comma **10.** early,

P. 95 COMMAS FOR INTRODUCTORY WORDS 1. Goodness, **2.** Yes, **3.** Well, **4.** Darn, **5.** Oh, no,

P. 96 COMMAS FOR DIRECT ADDRESS 1. Donna, **2.** You, Don, **3.** window, **4.** expression, Dan, **5.** But Don, **6.** none

P. 97 THREE POSITIONS FOR DIRECT ADDRESS Samples: **1.** What are you looking for, mister? **2.** Dad, what do you need for Father's Day? **3.** Listen, my children, and you shall hear.

P. 108 SUPPLY PUNCTUATION. Well, Jerry, wife, menagerie? strapping, handsome. Goodness,

withered, Jer, hunched, you. years? say, out, pal?

Cast Your Spell   pages 98–107

After completing the exercises in this chapter, you should

- understand the image-creating power of spelling
- gain proficiency in building habits of good spelling by
  visual concentration
  kinesthetic experience
  correct pronunciation
  recognizing silent letters
  making associations
  following rules for plurals: +-s, +-es, f to v +-es, root changes, no change
  learning to form contractions, especially the *have* contraction
  studying individual troublesome words
- be able to compose sentences using words that employ these methods.

P. 99 MEASURE YOUR SPELLING ABILITY. 1. quiet **2.** misspell **3.** occurred **4.** forty **5.** already **6.** all right **7.** principal **8.** mathematics **9.** lose **10.** choose **11.** friend **12.** your **13.** it's **14.** surprise **15.** equipment **16.** disappoint **17.** clothes **18.** medicine **19.** fourth **20.** forward **21.** separate **22.** their **23.** Wednesday **24.** pedal **25.** brakes **26.** business

P. 100 SAY THE WORD.
1. mischievous, grievous, disastrous
2. remember, hinder, enter (The er in each word is shortened to r.)
3. realize, really; liable, grammar, attendance, weird, Halloween **4.** Halloween (It is a holiday) **5.** Root words: mischief, grief, Hallow's Eve, real, athlete, hurry, convene

P. 100 SUPPLY SILENT PARTNERS. wrath, wring, wriggle, wry, wrote, writing, wrestle, written, wrong, wretch, wren, wreck, wreathe, wrap, wrack, wrangle, wrist, wrenched

P. 101 FILL IN. 1. wry **2.** wrote **3.** wrestling **4.** wrapped **5.** wretch **6.** wriggled **7.** wrath **8.** wrist **9.** wrenched **10.** wrong **11.** written

P. 102 LEARN TO FORM PLURALS. coats, shoes, Joneses, cats, babies, bushes, windmills, three-year-olds, mothers-in-law, monkeys, Stetsons, wives, chiefs, geese, Japanese, deer

PP. 102–103 WRITE PLURALS. taxes, birches, thrushes, cannisters, mothers, houses, benches, bicycles, dashes, schedules, processes, Misters Ford, circuses, dresses, branches, hoaxes, addresses, refugees, choirs, immigrants, waxes, scratches, bricks, pouches, witches, sashes, foxes, geniuses, planes, keys, Smiths, classes, pictures, Davises, occupants, caresses, crashes, hairbrushes, locks, stitches, sandwiches, prefixes, actresses, cents, latches, brushes, hurrahs, atlases, wishes, ditches, masses, dishes, tickets, watches, patients, Misters French, matches, eyelashes, sixes, grasses

P. 104   PLURALIZE THE FOLLOWING.   tariffs, show-offs, footballs, feet, trout, sheriffs, Japanese, women, jackknives, mice, children, loaves, old timers, dwarfs, lives, wives, elves, hoofs, hooves, tap dancers, moose, halves, selves, housewives, griefs, giraffes, calves, handfuls, wisdom teeth, men, geese, leaves, by-lines, passers by, thieves, knives, godchildren, cupfuls, onlookers, fish, sheep

P. 104   FILL IN THE SLOTS.   1. thieves **2.** chefs **3.** loaves **4.** calves **5.** teapots **6.** safes **7.** handkerchiefs **8.** scarves **9.** footprints **10.** leaves **11.** feet **12.** teenagers

P. 104   1. firemen **2.** children **3.** bystanders **4.** men **5.** women **6.** nightshifts **7.** firefighters **8.** two-by-fours **9.** roofs

P. 104   1. tradesmen, **2.** wharfs (wharves), **3.** beefs (beeves), **4.** onlookers, **5.** Germans, **6.** Japanese, **7.** Chinese, **8.** Swiss, **9.** Portuguese, **10.** species

P. 105   MAKE THE WORDS PLURAL   1. taxes **2.** brushes **3.** scratches **4.** patients **5.** atlases **6.** washclothes **7.** lamps **8.** waltzes **9.** strifes **10.** firemen **11.** houses **12.** cupfuls **13.** times **14.** widows

1. churches **2.** floods **3.** papers **4.** puffs **5.** crutches **6.** addresses **7.** deer **8.** prefixes **9.** chiefs **10.** men **11.** eyelashes **12.** desks **13.** gulfs **14.** sheaves

P. 105   CONTRACTIONS   1. wasn't **2.** weren't **3.** don't **4.** doesn't **5.** didn't **6.** hasn't **7.** haven't **8.** hadn't **9.** shouldn't **10.** couldn't **11.** mustn't **12.** wouldn't **13.** mightn't **14.** oughtn't

P. 106   *HAVE* CONTRACTIONS   1. you've **2.** we've **3.** I've **4.** would've **5.** could've **6.** should've **7.** might've **8.** must've **9.** may've

P. 106   WRITE THE CONTRACTIONS.   they'll, she's, Jim's, here's, there's, who's, it's, you'd, Bob's, he'd, she'd, we'd, they'd, we're, they're, how're

P. 106   SUPPLY THE CONTRACTIONS.   1. can't, He's **2.** didn't **3.** he'd, won't **4.** Bob's **5.** It's **6.** Jane'll **7.** aren't **8.** should've **9.** Isn't **10.** Where's

Index